WAKI

WITH

MOTIVATION

CURE PROCRASTINATION

INCREASE PRODUCTIVITY

AND

WIN YOUR WAR

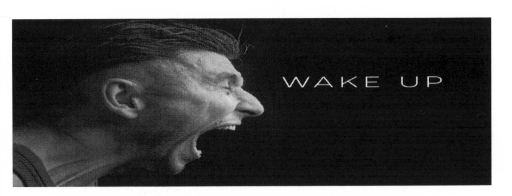

ELIMINATE NEGATIVE, STAY HUNGRY,

DISCIPLINE YOURSELF, STOP BEING LAZY,

TAKE ACTION AND FINISH WHAT YOU START

TABLE OF CONTENTS

INTRODUCTION

For most of us, accepting 100% responsibility for everything, both negative and positive in our lives, is a really difficult concept to embrace. We look at our lives and still feel like victims, where it feels impossible that we are responsible for things over which we feel like we had no control.

Things like a motor vehicle accident or being on the receiving end of a right sizing or downsizing exercise at the company we work at. How could we possibly be "RESPONSIBLE" for either of those two incidents?

It is for this reason that I want to change the term from "Take Responsibility" to an easier one to accept and adopt, namely "Take Charge". The concept of us taking charge of our lives and accepting that unless we take action to change things, everything will stay the same and we will remain trapped in a downward spiral.

When we accept responsibility for everything, both good and bad, we take charge of our lives and we empower ourselves to make the positive changes we need in our lives. The moment you take charge of your future and stop avoiding responsibility, you liberate yourself from a culture of blame and shame and you put your power back in your hands.

After taking charge of your future and accepting that the way things are going to turn out, is in your hands, you are once again in the driving seat.

As long as you look at your life and blame your circumstances on the state of the economy, the president, bad luck or any external factor, over which you have no control, you are a victim of your circumstances and you are trapped, with no option to make things any better.

The moment, you accept that you are responsible for your past and everything, which has happened until now, you realize that you can mold your future, shaping it just the way you want to. Simply by taking inspired action daily, which will over time help you to develop the knowledge, skills, uncover the necessary resources and turn you into the type of person you need to be to attract the level of success you desire.

Discipline is the bridge between where you are right now and where you want your life to go in the future. As soon as you take charge of your life and decide what you want in your future, create a crystal clear written down vision and stop looking for instant gratification in the moment.

The path to success is paved with the short term pain of daily discipline, which weighs ounces, versus the massive pain of regret, which comes from continuing down the slippery slope of neglect. Remember that the way you do anything is the way you do everything.

Those small slips in your daily commitment, where you make small concessions in your routine, will over time drag you back into your old comfort zone of neglect.

Decide what actions you need to take daily and build a new set of behaviors or habits to support you to carry these out daily. It will initially take a lot of willpower and discipline to carry out all the new activities, but after about 90 days the new routines will become entrenched and be an integral part of success habit set.

You have a set of habits right now, which are keeping you trapped in a life you don't enjoy. Don't you think it is time to replace them with a set of success habits, which will propel you to the level of super achievement, you know you are capable of achieving. Daily discipline, sustained over time, has the potential for creating miracles in your life.

You don't need to completely reboot your life and start over. Where you are right now is the perfect place to start. A few well-chosen new daily routines or behaviors, which require you to apply your willpower to carry out every day, will have a massive impact on how your life will turn out in the short, medium and long term.

The feeling of accomplishment, you feel every day once you have successfully carried out all your new daily routines or new behaviors, will build your self-esteem and confidence. Review your progress daily and reward yourself with a feeling of satisfaction for meeting your commitments to yourself, every day.

Accept 100 % responsibility for your life and begin to believe in yourself and your potential. Taking charge or said another way accepting 100 % responsibility for your future, is one of the highest forms of maturity and the only way to make any positive lasting and meaningful changes to your life.

Once you show a real willingness to be accountable, you take charge and accept that the only person, who is going to build the future you want, stares back at you from the bathroom mirror each day. You empower yourself and put the power to build the future you want squarely in your hands.

Happy Reading!

CHAPTER 1

MOTIVATION

Motivation is one of those intangible things in life that many have a love/hate relationship with. One day you may start your morning fully charged and overflowing with motivation to tackle whatever the day brings you, and the next you may wake up feeling completely drained, wishing you could just stay in bed for the rest of the day.

While we all have dreams and future goals that we want to achieve, why is it so hard to get motivated? Getting motivated to succeed is a tricky thing, but if the right steps are taken, it can be achieved.

First, you need to think about what you want to achieve or obtain in life. Be sure to include every goal no matter how big or small. Then you need to visualize these goals. Find and cut out actual pictures of these goals and put them somewhere you will see them everyday.

Some people create a "dream board" by placing these pictures together on a bulletin board. You will be motivated daily by seeing real pictures of your dreams each morning.

Once you have determined what your goals are, you need to write down smaller goals that, once accomplished, will bring you a step closer to achieving your big goals.

Sometimes it is even necessary to break these small goals down even further into detailed to-do lists. For example, if one of your dreams is to build a home in 10 years, then you need to determine how much the home is going to cost to build.

Once that is done, divide the total cost by 120 months to determine how much extra you should be saving every month to ensure you will be able to start building on time. Now, you need to create a list of mini steps to take daily that will help you reach your monthly goal. Once you do this and start seeing results, you will stay motivated.

You will not continue to stay motivated if you do not reward yourself for achieving those little goals that will eventually bring you face-to-face with your dream goals. A reward can be as big or small as you want to make it.

For instance, it can be taking a break to enjoy a good book or even treating yourself to a massage. By setting rewards for yourself, you are giving yourself daily, weekly or monthly incentives to keep you motivated to cross off those mini to-do lists and achieve your dreams!

With topics that we experience on a daily basis, for example education or language, we often think we know a lot about them because they are so familiar, and yet they are really so familiar because they are so important; and part of their importance derives from the fact that they are huge topics with innumerable aspects, angles and depths which make it virtually impossible for anybody to truly say they understand it fully.

To take my first example, education, we all feel we know plenty about it, for we all went to school, experienced teachers, and did examinations - to mention three core elements - but any cursory investigation into what education is and how it is best propagated and implemented rapidly reveals what a complex issue it is.

And so, too, for motivation; we all encounter motivation and need motivation, but most people are extremely hazy about its qualities and properties and how best to develop it. I would like, therefore, to comment on one of the least noticed aspect of motivation!

The first thing to notice about motivation, which is not obvious until you report it, is that motivation is invisible. You cannot 'see' motivation. This fact has very important consequences. First, as the saying goes, 'out of sight, out of mind'.

Yes, it is also true that we are aware of motivation on a daily basis in the sense that the top soccer team in the league seems to have a lot more of it than the also-rans, or that Richard Branson or the late Steve Jobs seem to have a lot of motivation.

Or that waking up in the morning one feels lousy and about to go to work and one wishes for more motivation; but that is all on the surface: we are not really thinking about motivation and its qualities; we are noting its effects.

So the fact that we do not see motivation means, especially in an organizational context, that we do not give it due time and attention. There is a parallel here with other things that are 'invisible': our values, for example, and to give one paramount value, love. As Denis Burkitt observed, "Not everything that counts can be counted."

Getting motivated to succeed is difficult when you do not have a plan in place to help you achieve your goals. While there are numerous of other things you can do to help you get motivated, it is important that the three ideas above are incorporated in your plan. They will not only help you get motivated to succeed, but also to stay motivated.

CHAPTER 2

Some people wake up with the lack of enthusiasm. They do not want to pursue their life as they should. They do not have fun for their being and see no meaning to go on. They see all the problems instead of opportunities.

They focus on how bad situation they have been through. The worst of all is that they are bored with their life. They do not feel the juice of living further. In this article, we will talk about how to be motivated using the law of attraction.

In order to be motivated in life, we need to have a certain mindset. You must have had some days in the past that you feel so happy. You couldn't even wait to wake up in the morning. You had all energy and enthusiasm.

What made you feel that way?

It is some condition that you plant into your mind in that period. You must have had some favorable event that you were looking forward to and you were excited about it. How are you going into that state again? Here are some simple tips to give you motivation by using the law of attraction.

1. Have your goals set.

Before you do anything, you need to know what you want out of it. You have to know your purpose. It is impossible to wander around without having the direction. You need your goals set so that you know where to go and what to do.

This simple process will make you more advance than others and make you more fun in living. Decide what you want now and have it written to be your master guide. In short, you need goals to be motivated.

2. Take a look at your goals first thing in the morning.

Look at your goals and expect the result of the achievement will give you the power of living. You can rewrite your goals to communicate with your mind on the importance of the goals.

Once goals are seen, your reticular system in your brain will work to align you into the direction in harmony with your goal achievement. This is one of the methods of using law of attraction.

3. Feel gratitude on what you are having.

You have to be happy with what you already have. No matter what condition you are in, it is already good for you. You have all advantages or power within you.

Feel thankful to your parents, your family, your spouse, your friend, your kids, your teacher, your students, your bosses and your spiritual guide who make you here. Feel thankful to everything. Once the feeling of gratitude come up, you will have no worry or fear in your living. You will feel more confidence in facing the world.

4. Make positive affirmations.

Think of what you want. Ask yourself who you need to be in order to get those. Find out what type of the person you want to be in order to achieve your goals. Make a few of short sentences for your affirmation.

Something like I am an excellent salesperson. I am a leader. I am a great father. I am the best. When you say it, you need to feel it in your soul. Feel the vibration that happens.

Tony Robbins suggests that adding the intense tone into your voice and intense physical movement and facial expression will increase the power of affirmation. He called it incantation. You can make use of his method and you will feel more juice in your day.

5. Visualize what you want.

Visualization is to see what you want happens within your inner eyes. You find a quiet place without disturbance. Sit comfortably and close your eyes. Then you visualize the situation that you achieve your goals and receive all benefits out of it. See what happened to you at that circumstance as it is happening in front of you. What will you feel?

Visualize every morning will attract the situation and attributes that are favorable to your goal achievement according to the law of attraction. You can accelerate your attraction by adding some background audio onto your visualization. Attraction Accelerator can be one of your choices.

CHAPTER 3

DISCIPLINE AS THE KEY TO MOTIVATION

Motivation is a fleeting state that requires a certain mental or emotional approach to reach a goal. It fluctuates depending on outward conditions.

In contrast, discipline can help you conquer the toughest challenges. For example, you may wake up with a cold or flu and have a 10,000 word report to write, yet not be motivated to complete it. However, discipline commands you tackle the work knowing it must be completed, regardless.

Success depends on discipline because motivation comes and go. It entails chipping away at a goal until the desired outcome is realised. Motivation is interrupted by excuses and fades steadily. This is why your motivation at the beginning of the year contracts towards the latter part.

"In other words, if you are an effective manager of yourself, your discipline comes from within; it is a function of your independent will. You are a disciple, a follower, of your own deep values and their source.

And you have the will, the integrity, to subordinate your feelings, your impulses, your moods to those values," states author Stephen R. Covey in The 7 Habits of Highly Effective People.

You mustn't wait until the perfect conditions to begin a task. Rather, tackle it boldly until the conditions become perfect. Motivation is an overused word, apparent in the corporate world where managers try desperately to inspire their employees.

Yet, in the sporting world motivation cannot be relied upon by athletes for success. Winning athletes know discipline is the cornerstone of success. They consistently show up to training when they're less inclined. Unforeseen circumstances may interrupt their preparation, yet they are determined to put in hours of dedicated practice.

Life has a way of dragging you every which way if you let it. This means if a crisis or unplanned event arises, you may be unmotivated to take action on your goal. This scenario happens all too often.

If you think back on the previous week, did something unexpected affect your motivation?

Did it wane during the week or were you disciplined despite the interruption?

By carefully studying your environment and analyzing your daily frustrations, you'll find that opportunities for disruption start to jump out at you. Daily discipline is the key to this exercise.

Get Feelings Out Of The Way

You must disassociate feelings with actions to reach your goals. This is the biggest impediment affecting people because they are dictated by their emotions, instead of seeing the goal as the prize.

You will enjoy reaching your goals more than the immediate gratification of succumbing to your emotions. If you rely on feelings, you are less inclined to commit to the task at hand because you are dictated by short-lived emotional states.

Discipline means showing up time and again, irrespective how you feel. The goal has a greater purpose, so it is incumbent on you to stay committed until the end.

It's clear, you don't undertake a goal to play small. It's about winning and achievement that make the pursuit exciting. "The discipline of consistent action is what self-management is all about. It's the only way to win and keep winning,"

So, how can you be more disciplined and avoid counting on motivation?

First, create regular routines without over-committing in the early stages. If your goal is to exercise four times a week, build gradually instead of going all out in the first week.

The greatest impacts on your life will result from taking the first step and improving on it.

Gradual Improvements

In the sporting world there's a term known as, marginal gains popularised by Sky Team's cycling manager, David Brailsford. It is a concept referred to as the "aggregation of marginal gains." According to Brailsford it means, "The 1 percent margin for improvement in everything you do."

At the senior level, most professional athletes are of a similar ability in terms of: performance, dedication and skill. What separates first from second or third is the smaller gains, the 1% such as: sleep, nutrition and recovery.

The 1% increments add up, leading to marginal gains. Therefore, discipline becomes the means to success. "Success is actually a short race - a sprint fuelled by discipline just long enough for habit to kick in and take over," The key is to start small and make small increments towards your goal.

Second, discover your underlying motivation for pursuing the goal. Find a convincing reason to take daily action, even if it's the smallest task, you are likely to stay committed. People who have a compelling reason are disciplined until the goal is accomplished. The desire must be imbued with enthusiasm, you will stop at nothing to achieve it.

"As Samuel Johnson said, "The chains of habit are too weak to be felt until they are too strong to be broken." Anyone who thrives in any endeavour develops this discipline, the ability to be still, to stay the course, to grow down no matter what. No matter how the world receives them. No matter what results they get initially.

The forces of life conspire against you in the form of resistance. If you succumb, your efforts will be in vain and your success squandered. Yet, if you take them into account, you will stay resolute irrespective of the circumstances.

Persistent action in the face of fear is paramount. With this approach, you reinforce your self-esteem each time you commit to a task. When you discipline yourself, you're essentially training yourself to act in a specific way.

Stay with this long enough and it becomes routine - in other words, a habit. So when you see people who look like "disciplined" people, what you're really seeing is people who've trained a handful of habits into their lives."

Discipline replaces motivation because you show up consistently. The goal is too important to allow feelings to get in the way. We must all suffer one of two things: the pain of discipline or the pain of regret."

CHAPTER 4

DISCOVER WHAT MOTIVATES YOU

There is no "one size fits all" when motivating individuals. What I deem as a motivating influence, may not be important to you; however, we all require some level of motivation. Even highly motivated people need stimulus along the journey.

What and how to provide that stimulus, depends on having more than a working knowledge of your people. Good leaders have a genuine interest in each member of the team, and provide tailor-made motivation consistent with each ones needs and desires.

The key factor in motivating others is to "influence behaviour". Achieving organisational goals are dependent on mobilising individuals to achieve pre-determined and strategic outcomes. The longevity of such, is dependent on the retention and inspiration (outworked via motivation) which team members show.

So what motivates you?

There is no right or wrong motivator, as we must keep in mind that the reason for providing motivation is to influence behaviour. These changes in behaviour serve a common purpose or organisational outcome.

As mentioned earlier, none profit organisations provide an ethos, belief or objective which is central to its cause. Providing tangible evidence of advancement, positive change and outcomes are the lifeblood to motivating its people.

Here are some key motivators which influence behaviour.

Reward

Providing a means of reward or incentive is perhaps the earliest form of motivation we experience. As a child, we are exposed to the "carrot and the stick" mentality. Behave in a certain way and reward is ours. "Eat all your veggies and you can have desert".

"Go straight to sleep and if you're good, I will buy you that toy". As an adult, the means are a little more refined but the methodology is the same. Hit the targets and you get a bonus, pay rise, promotion etc.

Outcomes

A key motivation to many, is the visible sign of completion. Many of us are motivated by "seeing" the end result achieved. Finalising goals and outcomes are a satisfying reward and sense of personal and corporate accomplishment.

Taking a project to completion is immensely satisfying and perhaps one of my favourite motivators. Celebrating completion is reward for many, and regardless of how that is outworked, it's motivating influence is immense.

Positional - Influence

Leaders have a desire to influence, and often the position one holds provides opportunity for such. Whilst some of the greatest influences in history have done so without a recognised position, most of us still respond to title rather than function.

Influence can be achieved in many ways, it is sufficient in this chapter to acknowledge that the need to control the behaviour of others is often achieved through the medium of position. Those who perceive such a medium as an hierarchical power base, are often motivated to progress through and by it.

Personal Growth

Training and development serves several objectives.

It ensures organisational consistency and purpose

It produces an environment for personal development and a recruitment base, which can impart organisational vision and values.

It provides a stringent measurement for quality control and strategic timeframes.

It harnesses talent and assimilates it into organisational growth and development for the foreseeable future.

Individuals with a desire to receive ongoing training in specific skills, have a passion to future proof their careers, and will often forgo other motivating factors in order to grow personally.

Belonging

Being a part of something larger than oneself, is a key factor in choosing which organisation gets out investment. Without doubt, one of the greatest motivators within none profit organisations is a sense of belonging.

Being a recognisable part of the big picture and playing ones part is a significant motivator to many. It's not an issue of whether people will invest their skills and talents, but where. Providing an environment to belong goes way beyond other motivators.

Fear

As politically correct as the world is today, fear is still used to control behaviour and outcomes. I often encounter such methods, where heavy tactics are used to increase input and maximise effort from workers.

Fear in itself is insufficient to control, for without the threat of consequences it is a shallow motivator. Failed objectives, poor productivity or results, outsourcing, turn down in the economy, redundancies, termination, salary reductions, and demotion are all used to motivate change in behaviour.

Love

Last but far from being least, love is powerful. The Greeks defined the term love in four ways:

Agápe, Éros, Philia, Storge

Whichever expression one experiences love, its motivation is expressed in powerful ways. Love is not limited to emotion, but action. When one "acts" with genuine concern or love for another, it motivates all manner of loyalty and behavioural change.

We are more responsive to love in action than words.

People will "go the extra mile", support, invest, uphold, protect and even fight for the family vision because of it. Loyalty that is expressed in the loving appreciation of another's efforts is a compilation of all other forms of motivation.

Genuine consideration for those around us, is the most primal yet powerful form of motivation. Those motivated by it, will inspire in others a similar motivation.

When all other motivators are ineffectual, love has the capacity to build hope, confidence and assurance in the future. It may not change the company's bottom line, but it will change our greatest resource.

CHAPTER 5

HOW TO STAY MOTIVATED THROUGHOUT YOUR HECTIC SCHEDULE

It is not uncommon to find oneself in a situation, where staying motivated is just not possible. It is one of those things that seem so out of control and it happens at crucial moments, making it something we may (or may not) regret later. So the key question in such a situation would be, "How does one stay motivated?"

If you've ever had a goal or a dream, you know that simply desiring it, is not enough. Irrespective of what your object of desire may be, it is easy to fall in love with it, but when it comes to obtaining it, that's no walk in the park. And this is where the motivation and your motives, come into the picture.

You see, when you started to desire, all you saw was your want for something and that thing itself. The psychological realization of all the obstacles that lie in your path, don't occur immediately. The reason it happens in that order is because we are ultimately (social) animals. We see, we want, we get. End of story.

But in life, that concept doesn't always apply. In life there are other concepts that come into play, like struggle, competition, hindrances and what not. All these things are blows to the mind.

The mind, which naïvely thought that simply wanting something was enough, starts to realize that there are many other forces acting against it. It begins to see the 'price' it has to pay, to get to the objective.

Slowly but steadily, the motives begin to lose their initial charm. Mind you, the desire is still very much there; but for some unexplainable reason, the drive seems to go missing. Suddenly, it is only the wanting part which remains. That's because ladies and gentlemen, motivation has left the building.

If you recall, it is pretty clear in the definition that motivation is simply two things, a change in behaviour and the existence of a motive. The moment one or even both these things cease, motivation ceases.

Finally, we can come to the last and most motivating part of this whole story,

"How does one stay motivated?"

The million dollar question. How does one, not lose sight of the goal and keep charging towards it without losing drive?

Fortunately, the answer is far less dramatic and far easier to understand and apply. Stated below are a few of the most tried and tested methods to stay motivated irrespective of what the situation might be.

1. Write down the goal

How many times have you started out something, with enough motivation to rule the world and less than a week later, you're asking yourself, "Why did I even start doing this in the first place?" And when you don't remember the reason, what do you do? You, quite obviously, quit.

We assume that if we don't remember, it is simply because the reason was not strong enough in the first place. That my friends, is the first step to becoming unsuccessful.

The moment you have a goal, clear out all the extra information in the background and then write down the core reason why you are doing or going to do it. Leave no room for ambiguity. Every time you see that piece of paper and read your goal, it must be clear and it must hit you in the right spot (heart).

2. Divide and Conquer

Since time unknown, the world's greatest rulers have used this strategy and won battles. From Julius Caesar to the British Empire, everyone followed this strategy. Then why shouldn't we?

There is a famous adage, "Rome wasn't built in a day"

It emphasises the importance of giving things time. Rushing into something is easy, rushing out, not so much. You need to understand what all steps will be involved in achieving your goals and then divide those steps into smaller time periods.

For example, let's say you decide to lose 10 kgs. That isn't going to happen, with the regular exercise and diet method, in 1 day. In most scenarios, it won't happen in 1 month either.

But if planned properly and divided into smaller achievable targets like, 1kg in 5 to 7 days, you have a pretty good chance of losing 10 kgs in 2 months or maybe even more.

So the idea is simple. Divide the steps to achieve the ultimate goal, into small periods. Then one by one, you can take down all the steps and conquer it.

3. Understand and accept all possible outcomes

In one word I mean be 'rational'.

More than often, we lose motivation because we don't understand that some things are not going to happen no matter what we do. There exists some loophole that may pull our goal out of our hands. But that does not mean we stop trying.

You want to be the first ranker in a competitive exam. Will you stop trying simply because there is a possibility, that someone somewhere has photographic memory and is also going to write the same exam? No, right?

In that spirit, you need to stay open to all the possibilities. You may come within inches of winning and lose Or you may have every chance of losing and still end up winning. Why discount that?

4. Lose the pessimism

There's a saying, "A pessimist is someone who, when smells flowers begins looking for a grave."

Nobody, I repeat, nobody can help someone who has decided in advance that they are going to lose. You can take the losing horse in a race and make him a winner; but a horse that refuses to run, has no future.

Pessimism is that one disease which can turn the most capable person into an absolutely worthless person. So there is really no room for motivation in a mind where pessimistic thoughts breed. The moment you take an optimistic approach, motivation will follow.

5. Surround yourself with motivation

If you sit in a room full of sad, sobbing people, it is natural that you'll end up feeling depressed. It's plain logic, not rocket science.

Surround yourself with inspiring, motivated, happy, energetic go-getters and you will find it rubbing off on you. Because the human mind is a copycat. When the mind sees sad, it feels sad. When it sees happy, it feels happy.

Unless you are a sadist or a masochist, you will find yourself automatically feeling energised when in company of the energised. Read books about being motivated and biographies of successful people. Listening to songs that have fast beats also help.

6. Stop making excuses

Motivation is like that awesome friend; who when leaves the party, people begin to follow suit.

But you say, "No" Nobody leaves after the party. Why?

Because you need the party to end, so that the After-Party can begin..

You need to stop finding excuses to quit and start finding reasons to stay in the game. If you have 5 main motives to being with, add 5 motives that will act as the 'After-Party Motives'. Have a simple rule. You snooze, you lose. If you want something, you have to go and get it. So pick yourself up, dust yourself off and get the after-party started.

They said, "When you begin something, it is like bringing home a baby. Initially it is always fun and so amazing. There is nothing like it. But slowly as the wailing and sleepless nights begin, you feel exhausted. In such a scenario, you have the permission to question your abilities. But you don't have the permission to quit."

From then onwards, every project I've taken up, I've treated it like my baby. There are moments when I feel like it just can't be done anymore. But I go back to the drawing board and ask myself, "Are you going to quit on your baby?"

CHAPTER 6

HOW TO KEEP FOCUSED SO YOU CAN REALLY START GETTING WORK DONE

One of the things that most of us struggle with is keeping focus during the day, so that we can really start getting work done and we can start to be effective. Now, the reason this is, is because we've got so many things going on in our lives that we just can't stop thinking about everything.

If you can imagine our focus is like a computer, alright. Imagine during the day when we are trying to do our work and we've got so many things running through our head, Is like a computer trying to function with 1000 programs running.

For example, you might be worried about an argument you had with a loved one, or you might be stressing over all the work you have to, you might be thinking about how you have to walk the dog, or you just might be excited about something.

The result? We just can't focus.

So in terms of a computer just imagine your computer has got 1000 programs running at once. It's not going to really be able to execute the program that you're trying to use very effectively is it? It's not really going to be able to get that done.

So the biggest thing that you can do when trying to maintain focus and get work done is to eliminate all the multi-tasking and eliminate all the distracting thoughts in your head. So, here is a tip and a strategy that I use when trying to keep focus so I can really get work done:

Alright, you want to grab a piece of paper, just a blank piece of paper and a pen. And you want to take 15 to 10 minutes out of your day so that you can sit down and take everything that's going on in your head and put it down on the paper, just clear out your head.

So you might get 15 things, you might get 20 things, you might only get 10 things, whatever. You have just got to write down everything that's going down in your head.

So like I said it might be, oh you're worrying about that argument you're having with your spouse,; you're worried about all the other work that you've got to get done; you've got to walk the dog, you've got to pick up the kids from school.

Whatever it might be. You just have to write it down, just put it down on the piece of paper. The idea is to get all the things running in your head, out of your head, and onto the paper.

What that does is it clears your head and can give you piece of mind. So now you've got a list of maybe 15 to 20 to 30 things, maybe even just 10, on a piece of paper. You need to list them in order from most important to least important.

So most important might be finishing that report you've got to give to your boss or something like that and least important might be 'I've got to water my tomatoes'. Alright, because if you don't water those tomatoes it won't really matter that much, but if you don't finish that report, that's when trouble can arise.

So once you've listed them in order from most important to least important, you need to look at the ones at the very bottom, the least important ones and you just need to cross them off.

You just need to look at them and say, "Alright, I'm not going to do that today. I can't do that today. It's not important so I've just got to not worry about it." And you've got to mentally, consciously, let it go. Just let it go, so just cross it off.

So once you cross off the least important things that you really realize that you don't really need to do today, then you'll have a much shorter list.

Now what that list is, is a list of all the things that you can try to tick off. You have taken everything that is distracting you, pulled it out of your head, and put it on a piece of paper.

You can just relax a lot easier. So when you sit down to do your work, you're not constantly thinking about all the things that you have got to do. You can focus just on the task at hand, the most import things.

CHAPTER 7

HOW TO KEEP YOUR FOCUS FOR EXTENDED PERIODS OF TIME

To learn how to stay focused requires you to change the habits that shorten your attention span. After replacing some of your usual activities with activities that require more of your input you will be able to retain your focus for increasingly longer time periods.

There are many activities that negatively affect your ability to focus. You should eliminate as many of them as you can. This will increase your focus to a great degree.

The main focus killers

The main reason why people find it hard to concentrate on tasks is because they let their inner voice convince them how boring the task is and that they could be doing something more interesting instead. If you give in to your inner voice you will never be able to concentrate.

When you start ignoring such voice you will find it increasingly easier to concentrate. This happens because there will be no voice left in you telling how else you could be spending your time.

Also, watching TV greatly shortens your attention span. Quickly changing TV images make you into an impatient person wanting instant results. It takes time to accomplish tasks. However, TV watchers would rather do nothing than spend time on activities that require their full attention.

That is what observing fast changing images does to you. You will notice that if you stop watching TV your attention span will gradually lengthen. That will happen very naturally and will not require any extra work from you.

There are many other influences that shorten your attention span. The customer service gets faster, online checkout process becomes increasingly shorter, products that save people's time are the most popular ones. The society is gradually becoming less and less patient, wanting instant results no matter where they are or what they do.

Instant results are good because they save time, but this can backfire if you need to accomplish something. For example, if you are setting up your business, it will require at least couple of months of your constant attention.

However, if you are used to fast service and instant results, you will be demotivated to keep focusing on your business because you will not see any evidence of success during its early stages.

Prepare yourself for focus

If you want to learn how to stay focused you should replace activities that produce instant results with activities that require some time to accomplish. For example you can replace watching TV to reading books.

You can replace online games with some activity that takes time, like painting, for example. This will make you understand how to stay focused without putting too much pressure on you. It will be like a game rather than a chore.

Also, if you take your car everywhere, try walking longer distances than you used to. A great way to learn how to focus is to bring consciousness into your everyday activities. When you are absolutely in the moment it is always easy to focus.

The best example of being in the moment comes from children and animals. When children play they are totally conscious of everything about the game. The animals are absolutely conscious in every moment because they do not have the ability to logically think. You can learn a lot by just simply observing animals and children.

So next time you are trying to accomplish some task, you should be entirely present. If you need to write about something, you should be completely involved in writing and not let your mind wondering off.

Also organized surroundings can really help you stay focused. When you clear your desk you remove most possibilities for external distractions. If you are doing some project on your computer you should not open more browser tabs or any other programs than you need.

Meditation is a great method to understand how to focus because when you meditate you learn to be still for increasing periods of time. Once you learn to be still during meditation, it will be easy for you to bring that stillness into your daily tasks.

The focus time

You should always define a clear outcome of any task before actually undertaking it. Otherwise you will waste your energy without getting anywhere. If the project is large you will need to note all the specific steps to take to get the project done. You should concentrate on one task at a time, complete it and then move on to another one.

You should also not forget to define the time when a particular task should be accomplished by and stick with this deadline. This is the idea behind the Parkinson's Law. It will explain how you can use your time in the most efficient way and get things done without using all your energy.

You should never attempt to accomplish important tasks when you are tired because they will never be done well. The best time to work on projects is early in the morning when your mind is still clear. If after waking up you still feel sleepy, you should take a cool shower and/or exercise.

This will wake you up completely and you will be ready for undertaking new tasks. This makes you understand that whilst learning how to stay focused you should pay attention to the times of your concentration.

To keep your focus for extended periods of time you should remove all possible distractions, even the tiniest ones. If you have long hair, you should put your hair into a ponytail; You should wear comfortable clothes.

You should work in a medium warm environment. If the workplace is too warm, you will become sleepy or get lazy. If it is too cold, you will keep thinking how cold you are.

It is important to make sure that you are working in a quiet place, where no one can distract you. It is better not to start any project whilst being hungry, because the thoughts of food will distract you for sure. Also if you eat too much you will get lazy, so overeating can be a focus killer too.

Whilst learning how to stay focused you surroundings should be very tidy and your phone should be switched off. You should not do anything else apart from the single task that you need to accomplish.

If you notice that you start getting thoughts that distract you, you should become conscious of the main task that you are trying to accomplish. This will eliminate off-subject thoughts and will let you concentrate on the main task.

Because people are so used to seeing and getting instant results, they become hopeless when it comes to accomplishing some task which requires more attention.

To tackle such problem you firstly need to prepare your mind for new concentration habits. You should replace your pastimes that produce instant results with new hobbies that take time to see the results.

After you have trained your mind to new activities you will be able to follow advice on how to actually retain your focus. This includes clearing your table before any project, putting away all the distractions and not letting your inner voice dictate what you should do.

CHAPTER 8

PRINCIPLES TO ELIMINATE DISTRACTIONS AND ENCOURAGE SUCCESS

We're all guilty of allowing the little things to distract us from what we should be doing. Instead of working, we chat with our friends or co-workers, check the latest chain email in our inbox, surf the internet, and do everything we can to avoid working.

Why? Because we don't feel like working - we're too busy daydreaming about being on the beach in Hawaii sipping a MaiTai or skiing the slopes. I'd like that too, but the fact is that in order to get where you want to be, you have to do the work required to achieve your goals and experience ultimate success.

Whether you are an employee or self-employed, your income depends solely on you. And the more efficiently you can work the bigger returns you will receive. Take a moment and ask yourself where you truly want to be?

Now ask yourself how many things you did today, yesterday, and the day before yesterday that directly contributed to the future results you want. And then ask yourself how many things you did today that did not contribute to your success. Those things probably distracted you from what you knew you should have been doing.

So you might be saying, ah - it's OK, everyone does it and shrug it off. Well, not everyone does it - however, most do. So what's the harm in the little everyday distractions? Those distractions are called distractions for a reason. They are distracting you from doing what you need to do in order to get you where you ultimately want to be.

Minimize distractions and you'll reach your goals faster - plain and simple. If you're self-employed and want to increase your monthly income by a certain amount, that won't happen by surfing the internet or playing solitaire.

It's going to come from doing the highest payoff activities that have the highest probability of building your success. You must minimize distractions and focus on the tasks that have a positive effect on your success.

Whether you are an employee, self-employed, or work at home, all of these ten principles can be applied to reduce and eliminate distractions.

1. Stay off the internet. Just don't get on it - because once you do, you're more likely to get sucked into it. If you have to get your fix, do it at the end of the work day or a set time during the day. Set a time that you honor - say, any time after 4pm and don't get on it before then, unless you absolutely have to.

2. Remove computer desktop icons. All of those things you love doing, like playing solitaire, just remove the icon from your computer desktop. Out of sight, out of mind is typically a good policy.

3. Remove desktop clutter. Magazines you say you're going to read on your lunch break and the picture of your sweetheart taped right to your computer monitor; these items need to be moved out of your immediate and frequent field of vision. It's OK to have personal items near you; they just shouldn't be right in front of where you look most of the time.

Only keep those items on your desk that you are currently working on. Anything else can cause a distraction and slow you down from getting your work done. Place only current files needed on your desk, while the others are filed away until you need them.

4. Eliminate noises. Listen to soothing instrumental music if you feel you need to listen to something, but talk radio or lyrical music will distract you from focusing on the task at hand.

Even alert sounds from your computer can be distracting; like the sound you hear when you receive an incoming email. Other distracting sounds can be the phone ringing, others talking, outside noise, etc.

5. Discourage walk-in traffic. Granted, if you're a manager it may be more difficult to do this; but if you can set specific times when you're available to talk and accept walk-ins, and times that you don't - it will help you to focus and complete tasks more efficiently.

Ideally, scheduling appointments is the most effective. For those who work at home, this rule applies to your family. Establish clear boundaries when you are not to be distracted, unless it's an emergency like the building is burning down and you need to get out.

6. Screen your calls. It's ideal if you have someone answer every call since real-person response is a vital part of a successful business. If this is a resource available to you, establish a schedule of when you are available to accept calls.

Outside of those times, you'll need to arrange a screening process to allow only the most important calls to make their way to you. I suggest reserving at least a few hours per day when you do accept any calls. Again, scheduling phone appointments is ideal and leads to working as efficiently as possible.

7. Ask for what you want. There is nothing wrong with asking for what you want. It's appropriate for all situations, but it must be done with tact and friendliness.

Busy professionals appreciate concise, focused conversation and you can show them you respect their time by not wasting it needlessly. Clear and concise communication saves time for everyone.

8. Learn how to wrangle in excessive conversation. Just as I mentioned in the above principle, everyone appreciates productive conversation. If you find yourself in a conversation with someone and it's not progressing to a point or conclusion, wrangle it in so you can get to a solution.

Again, this should be done politely and professionally but it's perfectly acceptable if you do. Superficial chit-chat is just that superficial. If you would like to talk to someone, at least have it be meaningful so it doesn't waste your time or theirs.

9. Work when no one else is around. This can sometimes be the greatest distraction elimination available. No clients, no co-workers, no phone calls. You can sometimes

accomplish more in 2 hours with no one else around than you can in 8 hours and a full office. Take advantage of alone time whenever you can.

10. Use and honor your calendar and task list. Last but certainly not least, this will help you stay on track and eliminate distractions. Remember; concentrate on doing the things that have the highest probability of you achieving your goals and that build your success. Distractions offer no return and no profit.

Wouldn't it be great if our 'good intentions' worked the way that we think they should? Not even enthusiasm guarantees positive results. There's often a wide gap between our intentions and our actions. We fail to take the action necessary to be in alignment with our good intentions. We allow things to distract us way too much each and every day.

Generally speaking, it's easier to become distracted when you're self-employed because it removes the accountability factor. When you don't have a manager looking over your shoulder, it's tempting to mess around with distractions.

Remind yourself that those little distractions offer little return, if any at all, for the time you've invested. Instead, stick to the productive tasks that build your success. Eliminate distractions and you have an even better chance of acting on your good intentions and achieving amazing results.

CHAPTER 9

REGAIN FOCUS AND END PROCRASTINATION

Procrastination can be a killer. Its "brother" distraction is just as bad. You can bet the reason these too are so powerful is because they are linked to fear. You know it. The main reason we lose focus and/or procrastinate is because we secretly think our goal is something we will fail at or, wait for it.

It's not crazy at all, and I'll talk about all that later, another day. I am going to show you how to recognize the severity and show you how to combat it. They say that awareness is half the battle so we are going to use that old chestnut to determine the depth of the issue.

Decide your goal - Whether you are going to write a page or two of your latest book or survey online resources for personal development, decide on a task you need to complete. Don't set a time limit; simply decide to work until you have completed the task.

Clear your Internet history - Every browser has a history button. It lists every site you have visited. Before you begin your task begin by clearing the history so that it shows nothing.

Begin your work and time yourself - Start your stopwatch and work as you normally would. Research and work to the best of your ability.

Review your results - Once you are finished stop your stopwatch and make note of the time. Use these guidelines to gauge your success.

How long did it take you reach your goal? - Note mentally all the times you stopped: Bathroom breaks, food, email checking, social media, texting and talking on the phone.

Review your internet history - Look at the sites you visited when you were "working". Did you check Facebook or Twitter? Did you get sidetracked by an ad (marketers LOVE when you do)? Or did you use the web to research your project. Go through each site and determine if it was a tool or a distraction. The history tells it all.

The goal for the next time you have the same task is to beat the time you just made. Consistent improvement is the goal.

There will come a time when you know exactly how long it actually takes to complete the task without distractions. Once you have that information you are ready to do the same for other tasks. Then the days are just one after the other of focused success.

If you want some help now to keep on task, these two apps will improve your times much quicker.

30/30 - This app helps keep you focused and on task. I'll let the site tell you more about it. The only drawback is that it's currently for iPhone only. But a stopwatch with a countdown timer will do the same general thing.

Anti-Social - This app allows you to set time for projects and blocks your ability to access any social media sites while you're working. You can also set as many web sites as you want based on the other distractions.

Focus is tough for many people. Of course, like everything, your success or failure is all mental. As I mentioned before there are some pretty profound reasons why people procrastinate and they do indeed have to do with your fears.

CHAPTER 10

MANAGING YOUR TIME TO STAY ON TASK

There are always going to be some days where, no matter how important the job (or sometimes because of how important the job is.), you are just having a hard time getting focused and staying on task.

Maybe you can't get started at all, you've gotten started but keep getting distracted, you're overwhelmed by the size of your to-do list, or you have several items of seemingly equal priority and aren't sure where to start. Here are some great ways to get (and keep) you moving.

1. When you can't seem to get started: Choose your task and think it through from beginning to end. Make a list of all of the tools necessary, and gather them together now - you don't want to build in interruptions by having to stop to get something.

Set a timer for 30 minutes, and 30 minutes only. For those 30 minutes, accept no interruption and work as hard as you can, with the agreement that at the end of that half hour, you can take a break, switch tasks, or keep going.

The majority of the time, you will have become so involved in your project that you will want to see the task to completion, but if not, make sure you honor your agreement with yourself. You can always repeat this process later, but in the meantime, you have accomplished some solid results.

2. When you can't seem to maintain focus: Work on a series of tasks in small bites of 15 minutes each. This is not as effective as the dedicated focus of tip #1, but some results are better than none.

After a couple of projects, you'll usually find a rhythm and start to settle in, but even if you go through the entire day in this manner, you will have made considerable progress on your list.

3. When you are overwhelmed by the length of your to-do list: Start by prioritizing your list, select the six most important, then commit to 60 minutes on each project. Set a timer, and switch when it goes off. This will keep you from getting so involved on any one project that you never get to the others.

Take a 10 minute break after each one, and give yourself a work-free lunch after item number three. This is vital to keep you fresh and energized for each new project, as well as to allow you to decompress and refocus. Note: some items will probably not require the full 60 minutes.

Switch when you complete that item. If you have time remaining for a second round, start with the project you initially got the farthest on, but did not complete, and repeat until all are finished. This will make a sizeable dent in your list. If you finish your list of six, make a new list.

4. DO take breaks, but schedule them by task rather than time. For instance, take a break after you finish project x, not at 11:00. Taking breaks at a scheduled time keeps you focused on the clock, instead of the task at hand, and as break time draws closer, you will mentally begin to disengage before the appointed time.

5. Work in a pattern of "little-little-big." We feel motivated when we see results, so by accomplishing two small tasks before tackling a large one, we feel like we're on a roll. When you've then finished the large task, returning to easy projects is a welcome relief.

This also ensures that your entire day does not mysteriously disappear into a vortex of minutia. We often intend to just "get the little stuff out of the way," and end up never getting to the projects of greater importance.

6. When you are looking for distractions, do your best to eliminate them. Turn off your email alerts, TweetDeck, and cellphone, unplug your land line, and put on headphones (you don't even have to play anything on the headphones, but they will keep people from talking to you.).

When your task is complete, give yourself 10-15 minutes to make the rounds and collect your various messages. Rinse and repeat.

CHAPTER 11

HOW TO BE MORE PRODUCTIVE AND ACHIEVE SUCCESS

Success may be happiness, job security, making a lot of money, or achieving a goal. Everybody's idea of success may be different. However, a way to get success for everyone is to be productive.

What exactly does productive mean?

Being productive is creating, producing abundantly, bringing about a result. Being productive and achieving isn't something that happens overnight.

You have to work hard, train yourself, have willpower, and have motivation. Being productive also means managing your time, having habits, following a schedule, focusing, being organized, and avoiding distractions.

If you live life being lazy it can actually be hard. You probably won't have a lot of money or success. If you live life working hard it can make life easier. You will be able to get most of the things that you want.

The following are a dozen steps to help you become more productive and therefore more successful.

1. Stop doing things that drain your energy and won't help lead to success.

Think about everything you do in a day. There is probably something that you do, that you might be able to skip without having any negative effects. Eliminating unnecessary things saves you time and energy.

2. If you don't have any habits, start one.

Pick anything that can help you in some aspect of your life. It could be waking up early, working out, pretty much anything. Give yourself about a month to master it. It will be hard, but don't give up. Habits help you develop a routine and a schedule which will keep you on time, and getting things done quickly.

3. Stop doing any bad habits.

Bad habits are a waste of time and energy. Stop doing them and make more time for starting new positive habits. A bad habit to stop is being messy. Disorganization is not good for being productive. So if you tend to have a disorganized desk, closet, or house change it. You probably waste so much time searching for things you need.

4. When you work avoid distractions and interruptions.

Don't constantly check your cell phone, e-mail and Facebook. You need to focus on whatever task you have at hand, not what your friends might be messaging you about.

Focus on what you're doing and you will actually get the task done faster. To keep your focus, don't answer phone calls. Set aside time to call people back later and also to check your e-mails. It's like having a designated distraction time.

5. Eat a healthy breakfast.

It sets a good tone to the rest of your day. Eating a nutritious breakfast will also help you stay full and awake. Also, make sure you eat lunch and dinner. You need to be physically and mentally energized. Plus, if your stomach is growling and you are hungry, you will be distracted.

6. Get plenty of sleep every night.

Some nights it may seem impossible to get enough sleep because you have so much to do. However, you need at least 7 hours of sleep. It keeps you energized so you are logically, emotionally, and physically ready for each day.

If you are tired, you will move slowly and it will be hard to think at full speed and be as productive as you can be. If you didn't get enough sleep the night before, make time for a short nap after eating your lunch.

7. Focus on one task at a time, don't multi-task or become distracted.

While multi-tasking seems efficient, it isn't always. In order to be most productive you should focus everything on one thing at a time. When that task is complete you can take a break and then move on to the next thing with complete focus. The more focus, the quicker and easier a task becomes.

8. Take breaks.

Working not stop will wear you out. You will feel so drained and you probably won't be very happy. Take frequent breaks even if it's only a break to stand up and stretch or to get a drink. You need at least a minute to relax before having to focus again. Plus, if you work at a computer it is good to give your eyes a break from the screen.

9. Practice a talent over and over until it is a great strength.

If you have a talent that can lead to success, take advantage of it. It may not be perfected so practice and practice until you are very good at it. Then use the strength to get what you want, to get success.

10. Manage yourself, to manage your time.

You can't stop time, you can't turn all the clocks back. So, if you want to have good time management skills, you need to manage yourself. Keep yourself focused, on track, and on time. Give yourself deadlines even if you really don't have any.

Avoid distractions that can use up your time and cause you to get things done late. Resist the urge to be lazy and procrastinate. Managing yourself takes a lot of willpower and it may take some time, but it can be done.

11. Use willpower to get things done, but not so much that you have none left.

Managing yourself and starting new habits will take some willpower. Using willpower is a good thing, but keep in mind that you can't use all your energy to force yourself to do something that you really don't want to.

If you spend so much time and energy forcing yourself into something, you won't even have any time or energy left to complete whatever it is. You have to slowly stop the resistance. This may take some time.

12. Try to keep yourself in check, emotionally and physically.

Sometimes your body feels energized, but your mind is just out of it. You can't seem to concentrate or do things right because you are upset or worrying about something else.

Then, there are other times when you want to do things, but your body is tired. You need to keep both sides of you in good shape. Sleep, eating, and exercise can help both your mind and your body.

You can even try meditation. Taking breaks is another way to keep yourself in check. These things are so important, but if you are conflicted it is very difficult to be productive. You need to use your different sides together to be your best and most productive self.

CHAPTER 12

ESSENTIALS OF FOCUSING AND TIME OPTIMIZATION

An adage of the modern age is that our attention span is the most limited resource available to anyone. With the multitude of possible daily distractions, learning how to hone in one's focusing abilities on the task at hand is essential for a healthy, productive lifestyle.

Learning these techniques is a product of practice and determination; the reward for dedicating yourself to them is that your results will increase and your focusing power will greatly expand. Several methods have been reviewed and proven to improve one's ability to improve workflow.

Becoming distracted, in essence, is removing yourself from the pattern or train of thought you were previously engaged in. All sorts of negative side effects can be associated with becoming distracted; most notable is the obvious: distractions lead to a lack of progress on the task at hand. Below is a small list of techniques to keep yourself on track and get more done.

Pomodoro Technique

This time-tested method has a very simple premise. You begin the cycle by setting a timer for 25 minutes, work those 25 minutes straight undisrupted, and then take a five-minute break.

After those five minutes are up, begin another 25-minute cycle and continue the cycle until you reach four total "Pomodoro's," or cycles.

The driving principle behind this method is that 25 minutes is a relatively short and manageable amount of time that most people can wrap their heads around and effectively tackle. Focusing power will exponentially improve.

COPE Method

Developed by productivity expert Peggy Duncan, this method is slightly more holistic than the POMODORO method. This acronym stressed: Clear-Organized-Productive-Efficient technique wherein the user must take a brief step back and examine the true causes of their distractions from a "10,000-foot" level.

Start this method with a notebook by logging activities that "hold you back from getting work done throughout the day" and analyze the importance of them.

Likely, you'll discover many superfluous activities that are neither essential or important. In order to achieve maximum productivity, cut these time-wasters out of your life and free up time for more important things.

Get Organized, Get Efficient

An often overlooked and underutilized method is a very simple one that everyone has access to. On every smartphone, laptop, and tablet there are two tools that form the foundation of your toolkit: Calendar and Reminder lists.

Begin by putting these tools at easy-to-access spots on your home screen and start to declutter everything else by utilizing the folders around it. Now, begin to plan every major event around your day whether it's going to the grocery store or exercising.

Every important work milestone should be planned and added to your reminder list. Begin every morning with a close look at your calendar and adhere to it with hourly check-ins. Boom. Productive.

Eisenhower Method and Pareto Analysis

The classic Eisenhower methodology utilizing a simple four-unit box to shift priorities and maximize efficiency. Steven Covey talks about this in his book: The 7 Habits of Highly Effective People. Separate a box into four equal spaces and list the following in them clockwise:

1. Urgent and important (tasks you will do immediately).

2. Important, but not urgent (tasks you will schedule to do later).

3. Urgent, but not important (tasks you will delegate to someone else).

4. Neither urgent nor important (tasks that you will eliminate).

Once completed, this box will help you visualize not only your priority list but how to determine if the distraction coming your way is a waste of time or not.

A healthy mind and body is an absolute essential in your personal and professional life. Remaining active with a combination of applicable cardiovascular training and endurance exercises will allow your mind to keep sharp and focusing on your tasks.

Productivity skyrockets after exercise due to the release of positive hormones associated with physical activity.

CHAPTER 13

EASY WAYS TO ELIMINATE DISTRACTIONS

Being able to do 10 things at once is useless if nothing gets done, and especially if nothing gets done right. If you can effectively deal with distraction and complete your most important piece of work, you'll be well on your way to success in any role you have.

Here are 14 ways to reduce or eliminate distractions:

1. Set a deadline

Give yourself a deadline and stick to it. When someone comes in you can say, "I have to get this report out by 2 P.M.. Can this wait until then?" You'd be surprised how well setting an artificial deadline can work.

It's like the old saying goes:

"If it weren't for the last minute, nothing would ever get done."

2. Use a Timer

Some people find their productivity jumps when they start using a timer. This works because you're setting a short-term deadline, but also because you are committing to doing your best work for a short period of time. Typical lengths of time would be 15, 30, or 60 minute blocks, but you can choose any length of time that suits your needs.

I use this technique with my primary mastermind group. We each have ten minutes to discuss our results and projections and look for suggestions. If anything more is needed, we book another time or do 1-on-1's. It helps us get through a ton of information in a short amount of time.

A countdown timer can be found online, as small program for your computer, or as a built-in feature on many cell phones.

3. Close your door

I'm a proponent of having an open door policy for management, but like any rule, there are times when it's beneficial to close the door and eliminate distractions. I suggest setting aside a 30 minute to an hour block of time where you can completely focus on any situations that need your personal attention.

Once everyone realizes that you're not to be disturbed during these short blocks of time, they will either take care of the situation themselves, or make a list of things to talk to you about after you're done your closed door session.

4. Private office

This is a technique I've used and love. It goes beyond simply closing your door. You actually find an office in a back corner somewhere, so you're not distracted by your phone and people don't really know where you are. This puts you out of the hustle and bustle of the everyday life and it's quiet too, so you're forced to work.

I'll usually take my laptop, turn off the Wi-Fi, mute the ringer on the phone (if there is one), and just start solving problems. Sometimes I'll take a huge sheet of flip chart paper with me, so that I can plan and prepare for any important activity that I'm working on. I love it.

5. Turn off email

I don't want you to freak out on me when I suggest this. I know you've probably already heard this tip a million times, but you've probably ignored it until now.

If you turn off your e-mail for an hour or two at a time, you will find a nice bump to your productivity. You won't be distracted by minimally important emails, and you'll soon realize that much of what you thought was URGENT, can probably wait an hour before being worked on.

6. Create an "Always Answer" list

Create an Always Answer list and then resolve to only take phone calls from those people when you're doing some focused work. You can call everyone else back in 20 minutes when you're done.

For instance, I'll always answer calls from my wife, even if it's during one of my time blocks. She knows how important my blocks of time are to me, so she'll keep the call short, make fun of me for being a productivity geek, and then say goodbye.

A list like this ensures that the people who need to get hold of you for something crucial are able to. Everyone else will just go to voice mail. You can return their phone calls at a later time.

7. White Noise Machine

Some people use white noise machines very effectively. They're the little machines (or programs on your computer/smart phone) that create a variety of sounds including waves, streams, thunder storms.

My wife and I use one when we have people over in the evenings. You see, my two year old daughter is a light sleeper so we often turn on the white noise machine in the hallway so it produces the sound of a babbling brook.

The background noise helps disguise distracting noises from us talking and helps keep her dreaming sweet dreams.

My friend Veronica swears by the "chirping birds" selection she listens to while she works.

8. Have a Scheduled Break to Do "Stuff"

Have a pre-made time to go around and take care of all the "not so important things" you'd like to do. This includes activities that aren't productive, but might be fun. You could go chat at the water cooler or head over to the coffee shop next door.

Ideally, you would put one of these "stuff" sessions after an important block of work. You can use it like a carrot to encourage yourself to work hard, since the fun will come as soon as you're done.

9. Make a list

If you're working and you suddenly remember an activity that has to be completed, simply add it to a list (computerized or pen and paper). Writing down a task does two things. First, it acknowledges the thought and clears your mind so you can back to work quickly. Secondly, it creates a list of important actions that you can work on later.

10. Find out What Distracts You

Different people are distracted by different things. Some stare out at the clouds, others keep checking Facebook status updates. Whatever it is, see what types of things distract you and simply eliminate them from your work environment.

11. Get Up Earlier

I've been getting up at 5 A.M. lately (that's early for me) and find it gives me extra time to get important jobs accomplished. The house is quiet and there's nothing going on to distract me.

I'm really more of an evening person, but I've found a lot of value in creating personal time in the morning. I remember when I used to work at 6 A.M.

It was nice to know that my day was officially over at 2 P.M. and then I could do whatever I wanted. This isn't for everyone, but you might want to give it a try. Believe me when I say it's hard at first, but if you can get used to it, you'll definitely get results.

12. Stay Hydrated and Properly fueled

Eat and drink before you go to work so your brain and body are ready to go. Visit the little boys'/girls' room to make sure you don't have any personal emergencies once you begin. If you'll be making phone calls, you might want to have some water handy, in case your throat gets dry.

13. Get off email/RSS lists

I regularly go through my RSS lists and trim any extra feeds that are no longer sending me relevant info. I've completely removed myself from any email newsletters. They are more reactionary and they clog up my inbox. Years ago I switched everything to RSS feeds. I still check them multiple times per day, but I can better control the content I'm viewing.

14. Write out a plan

Having a written list is an excellent way to avoid distractions. When you know exactly what you're going to do, it is much easier to do it. Besides, as you complete the various activities, you get to put a check mark beside it. That alone might keep you energized, because one of the most satisfying things a person can do is tick off a completed task.

CHAPTER 14

SETTING GOALS TO BOOST PRODUCTIVITY

Today is the last day of wishing there were more hours in the day. We all work hard and many of us definitely have had the feeling that no matter how hard we work it seems like either we haven't accomplished anything that day or there are simply just not enough hours in the day to get things done.

Well, read on and say goodbye to those days as starting tomorrow will start your most productive days ever with these steps.

We can all make time, we can all set goals and focus our minds on achieving them no matter how big or scary they may seem and the absolute kicker of this business called life is that we can be happy and calm and even enjoy every moment along the way.

If we choose to. Living with happiness, success and prosperity is a choice. Living with fear, angst, envy, misery and panic is also a choice.

I have researched the mystery that is the meaning of life by reading countless texts on positive thinking, on spirituality, on attracting the things that we all aspire to having in our lives. Many of those texts, or certain aspects of them, might be dismissed by people as being hyped up, over the top, or too airy fairy.

We are quick to assume that anyone who takes the time to reflect on the purpose of their life or the purpose within their life or, worse still, someone who admits to practicing some form of spirituality is a bit of a nut case; someone to be wary of.

In the past I have been as guilty of it as anyone else; avoiding eye contact with people I passed in the street who seem a bit too open and happy to be 'normal'. Maybe you think that some of the personal development or self-help information available is too idealistic for you.

Only hippies read that stuff right?

But if we remove the fear of not fitting within the framework that modern society has created, of being labeled 'airy-fairy', and just objectively evaluate the principles of achieving happiness, calmness, prosperity, successful relationships or whatever goal you have for your life, you just might find that there is more to your life than paying bills, watching television and accumulating 'stuff'.

Take action to move yourself further towards achieving what you want out of life. Identify, and by that I mean stop and really consider, the way your life is now.

What sort of daily routine have you established and what are the negative or non-productive things you are doing or thinking that are making you frustrated or miserable, that are holding you back from achieving what you want?

Maybe you, like many people, believe that you do not know what you want. Let's take some time to reflect on your life so far and try to isolate where your passion lies. What sort of activities or processes or behaviors make you feel proud and excited and full of life?

Every now and then we all have something special coming up on the calendar that makes us excited, that makes us want to spring out of bed in the morning. Let's try and find things that you enjoy doing that would make you feel that way every day.

Once you have identified your passion, and taken time to consider what drives you, then look at ways to help you set goals and take action to achieve them. If you have goals that you would like to pursue but have not taken any action on, think about why you have not taken any action. Is it fear? Don't be afraid to fail. Keep taking step after step.

For me, one of the biggest obstacles in achieving success in my own life was maintaining the momentum. I do not know how many times I have gained the inspiration to begin a particular project but then after a while my enthusiasm waned and my focus shifted and I found myself back in old habits, and ultimately being frustrated that I was not achieving what I wanted.

All your life you have always heard that you should set goals, but why? Well, because setting goals is a great thing and it will also boost your productivity and ultimately guide your success. Boosting your productivity is as simple as setting one BIG goal of actively participating in time management.

Here are a few steps that can boost your productivity no matter what you do.

1. When starting your day do your personal email first. Doing your personal email first will allow you to get this out the way and enable you to focus on the business of the day.

For business emails and etc. make a schedule of time to set aside for those emails. Also, make a schedule for some downtime to unfocus on business, you can use this time for your online time (i.e. surf the internet, play games, or pay bills) as well.

2. Now that you have handled your personal email let's get down to business. Second, to boost productivity start with the your least favorite and most tedious tasks.

These are the tasks most try to avoid for as long as they can therefore when time to do these tasks one has that "well I guess I'll do this now feeling". So, by doing your least favorite tasks and getting them out the way gives you room to have a more positive outlook on the rest of the day.

3. Next, focus your energy on the things that matter. In order to properly focus your energy make a to do list. When making your to do list put some thought into the tasks and the order in which your adding them because once you make the list you want to be sure to stick to that list as best as possible or you defeat the purpose.

Also, when making the to do list just add the things you need to do or are going to do for that day only.

So, make a new to do list for each day, I would recommend making a new list each day at the end of the day for the next or at the latest first thing in the morning of. Also, when making the to do list start with the least favorite tasks you have to do then put everything else on the list in order of time and priority.

4. Always do what is necessary, but always plan to do more. On your to do list always put on there and get done what is absolutely necessary for that day, but always add a few extra tasks that might not need to be done until the end of the week or so.

Adding extra items can be a great motivator and actually make you more productive by putting you ahead of schedule if you get to those tasks. Now, don't feel stressed to get them done that day, but after you complete the key things first then move on to the extras. Completing the extras can give one a great sense of achievement.

5. Next, you always want to be on time for appointments and meetings. You want to be on time and be known for being on time because being on time shows that you don't believe in wasting time (yours or anybody else's).

With that said being late happens to the best of us sometimes so no worries, but if you do have to be late just simple say excuse me I was held up, there is no need for a story.

6. Another step to take towards being more productive, try going into the office early at least once a week. Going in early can mean an office of just you and this gives you uninterrupted time in an empty office.

Going in early to an empty office can allow you to organize your to-do list for the day and get more things done. So, go in early and get everything lined up before there are any distractions to slow you down.

7. Being productive requires you to make the most out of your time and get things done. Everyone has things, just life in general that can cause distractions for them when trying to get work done.

So, in lieu of that, I suggest that you take a look at your schedule, to do list, and your whole day and identify those things/tasks that are really a waste of your time or a distraction to you and try to cut down on the time spent on those things/tasks until they are either eliminated or don't affect your productivity.

8. Lastly, be organized, create a schedule, and stick to schedules and routines. Being organized, ready, and sticking to your schedule can help you stay on track and improve your productivity. This can also cut down on the amount of stress that one has. Now, life

in general is stressful and not all stress is bad, but you can at least drop stress from not being organized and ready.

CHAPTER 15

EFFECTIVE WAYS TO BOOST PRODUCTIVITY IN THE WORKPLACE

One of the most effective ways to boost productivity in the workplace is to make your employees know and feel they are being appreciated and valued. A smile, a tap in the shoulder and words of encouragement can make a big difference. Follow these tips on how to motivate an employee:

Simple but powerful words are vital in employee-employer interaction. Simple and powerful words given to employees regarding their work is a very effective tool to demonstrate how much you value them.

"Please" and "thank you" are some words that you should do without when asking them to do a certain job. Once they perform their job very well, never forget to praise them with words like "great job".

Allot time for each person under your supervision. Meeting your target can easily be done if you spend quality time with the people who work for you. Take the time to talk to them and discuss their goals, their tasks, their progress and whatever setbacks they have working with the team.

Some managers spend at least an hour with each worker. Although not really much, but the short time can contribute a lot to the job productivity by letting the employees feel that you are directly involved in their work.

Goals should be shared. What the company is aiming and how to go about achieving this should be shared to every employee. This will give them a precise idea where they are going in working for you.

Never forget to schedule a regular meeting with the work force. These meetings are very important for them to voice their concerns regarding work and the management itself.

You will be quite surprise that through this interactions, you can learn a lot of things from your employees.

Positive motivation is a must if you want your company to be successful. This will give you a positive work environment that will make your business prosper. Learn how to be productive at work and you'll find yourself buzzing through the day happy, contented and accomplished.

But of course, with the number of distractions left and right, it's quite a tough task. Since you're reading this chapter, I assume that you're tired of spending days in your office without having much to show for it.

In that case, let me teach you how to be productive at work.

Step 1: Chuck Out The 3 Time Wasters.

Emails, Twitter and Facebook are three of the most unproductive time wasters you could ever come across.

Check your emails only twice a day (one in the morning and one in the late afternoon), unless your work requires you to constantly keep watch of incoming messages.

Avoid using Twitter, Facebook or any other social networking web site. I know it's hard to pry yourself away from these addictive past times, but you're not being paid to update your status or check how many followers you have accumulated since the last time you logged in.

Even just one tweet can derail your whole schedule, so stick to the no social networking rule. Unless it's actually part of your job description, stop logging in to these websites while at the office. Be strict about this and set boundaries for yourself. You can socialize or chat once you're done for the day.

Step 2: Remember Your Goal.

If you want to learn how to be productive at work, you must keep your eye on the prize. Remember when you were first hired? Didn't you want to get promoted, impress your boss and eventually make something of yourself?

By reminding yourself of the goals you have set, you are boosting your work morale. Don't be like the rest of the mindless drones who go to work day in and day out without really knowing why. You're different. You have a goal and this alone will make you more productive at work.

Step 3: Give Yourself A Deadline.

One advice I always give to those who seriously want to know how to be productive at work is to set a deadline. I'm not talking about the deadline that your superior gave you, but rather your own deadline.

By doing this, you become consciously aware of your decision to do your tasks efficiently. Of course, the output must not be sacrificed. Give yourself a reward for a job well done and learn lessons from the instances that you miss your personal deadline.

By learning how to be productive at work, you are paving the way to your own success. Your accomplishments today will be worth your weight in gold in the future. Besides, by being productive, you are not only developing your professional skills, you are also preparing yourself to take on bigger roles in the future.

CHAPTER 16

MAKING YOUR ROUTINE WORK FOR YOU

Everyone has a routine. Most times, I often hear, "I don't really have a routine" or "I haven't had a routine for a while". These are common statements from people that have come to the conclusion that because they weren't doing something often, they were out of the routine of doing it.

They are partially right. They may not be in the routine of doing it often, but they are in a routine. The routine is not doing it. The routine is doing other things instead of what they want to be doing. That puts them right in the middle of a routine. It may not be the routine they want, but it is still a routine.

Everyone has a routine. Everyone has habits and a schedule of things that make up a typical day. Control over these things varies and of course, no two people have the same schedule. The routine is there, no matter how much or how little you plan each day.

In the business world, this s is why some people are succeeding and others are failing. In the academic world, this is why some are acing courses and others are flunking out. And with health, It is why some are living a healthy lifestyle while others are not.

Those that are not living healthy can say, "I'm just not in a routine", but we know that they are simply in a routine that is not working for them. It may be working for someone else, but it is clearly not working for the person. If it was working for them, they would be reaching the goals that they have for themselves.

It sounds harsh, but it is the truth. Your routine is there. The only question to ask your self is:

Is my routine working for me or is it working against me?

If it is working for you, you must have put some time into setting goals, planning your actions so you could reach those goals. If it is working against you, you have two choices:

Choice 1: keep telling yourself you don't "have a routine" and pretend that your health will magically improve without you making any changes

Choice 2: take a look at your routine and change it so your actions match your desired result

It doesn't matter what area of life we talk about. The results that you see are completely dependent on the actions you take. We know that a business gets more customers with advertising and customer services strategies. We know that a student performs better on tests if they study the material beforehand. We also know that you will have a healthier life if you do healthier things.

So, take a quick look at your routine...you have one, you are in one and it is bringing you the results that you are getting right now. In fact, the routine you are in has likely been bringing your results for a long time.

If you are in a routine that is working for you, you know the results have been good. If your routine is working against you, well, maybe you should change something if you want your results to change.

CHAPTER 17

PRODUCTIVITY ROUTINE TO IMPROVE YOUR EFFICIENCY

I am sure that you are in a similar place to everyone else, where you feel like you are trapped on a daily treadmill, which does not seem to really go anywhere. All that seems to happen is that the treadmill speeds up and occasionally slows down, every day.

You feel like you are really working hard, but you never seem to have enough time to make those crucial changes you want in your life or to spend with your family. You arrive home exhausted every day, not feeling fulfilled or you feel like you have not really managed to achieve anything meaningful each day.

How would you feel about finding a system or rather a daily routine, which would help you to make significant improvements in your productivity, efficiency and effectiveness?

Not only will you get more of those meaningful life changing things done each day, which have eluded you until now, but you will also increase your sense of calm and get to feel like you have far more control over everything in your life.

After observing the massive amount of time I consumed every day, where I was constantly feeling overwhelmed, by the volume of work I needed to complete every day.

I decided there must be a better way of doing things and so I started searching for ways to get more done in less time and yet at the same time reduce the amount of stress and overwhelm I felt.

I have scoured every possible source of information I could find on productivity, met with experts in the field and after careful thought I have come up with a plan, which I believe works and will make a massive difference to your life and business.

There are a number of really effective ways to improve your productivity, but the one I want to share with you today, will help you to create a daily routine, which will gradually improve your effectiveness, efficiency and productivity. As you learn the new daily routines and they become an integral part of your success habit set, productivity won't be something you are pursuing; it will just become who you are.

Action Idea: When you wake up in the morning, don't push the snooze button to get another nine minutes of sleep every day. Try to wake up immediately and get straight out of bed. I call waking up and getting straight out of bed, my daily "activation energy charge".

It sets the tone for my day and programs my brain to be energized and able to tackle any difficult or challenging tasks, throughout the day.

The drive it takes to get straight out of bed in the morning sets the tone for the rest of the day, you feel energized and able to tackle any task, no matter how daunting, when you allow yourself to get that boost of daily activation energy first thing in the morning.

Once you have got yourself out of bed and you have energized yourself with your daily activation energy and you inspirational juices start flowing, don't rush straight into your day. Get yourself centered, by exploring your plan for the day, which you completed during your evening planning session, the night before.

The act of planning your day the night before allows you to apply a crucial principal in your life, namely the concept of "Done for the day" After you have invested a few minutes at the end of your day, to plan exactly how you will operate the next day.

You have a structure in your head, for how you will solve any challenges the next day and so you can give yourself permission to switch off from work completely and allow your batteries to start re-charging for the next day.

When you wake up in the morning, read through your plan for the day and allow yourself to get centered and grounded about everything you plan to do that day. During sleep, our minds are still very active and when you look at your plan for the morning, you may see a few tweaks, which would make your day flow even better.

This success ritual or new daily success routine, where you plan your day the night before, wake up, get straight out of bed, allowing your energy activation juices to start flowing and then you invest a few minutes to re-examine your plan for the day, sets the tone for a really successful and productive day.

I have included a few of my own daily sessions and new success habits as a guideline for you to create a daily productivity routine, which will suite your unique circumstances.

Wake up Early

I have found that there is no better technique for improving productivity, like waking up as early as possible and getting your day started with a bang. As soon as I wake up and I have centered myself and I am absolutely clear about how my day will progress.

I drink a huge glass of water to help my body deal with the dehydration, due to the long period since my last drink of water. This water helps me to cleanse my system, re-hydrate and energized my body. Dehydration is one of the greatest causes of loss of energy.

Some people suggest that you engage in some sort of physical activity before you start your day, to get your blood flowing. Try both options, one where you exercise to get your day going and the other where you start your day without exercise.

Your unique circumstances will dictate which one will work best for you. I have found that the early morning, is free from distractions and as such I get so much more done during the early hours of the day. I do not use any of this time for exercise.

I find I get the most value out of the early morning hours, if I tackle my toughest challenge for the day and get it done and dusted. There are no distractions in the early morning, so I can focus my entire energy on getting the tough stuff done first.

The feeling of accomplishment, which flows from getting the tough stuff out of the way early in the day also helps, set the tone for a fantastic day. It was Abraham Lincoln that first coined the phrase "early to bed, early to rise keeps a man healthy, wealthy and wise." No wiser words have ever been spoken about creating a life of success and meaning.

After getting the tough stuff out of the way, I then invest 20 minutes to meditate. This allows me to really settle my mind for the day and start the day with a clear mind, which is not cluttered by distraction. Meditation is unique to each individual, so how you do this every day is up to you.

I lie in a comfortable position, listen to various relaxing mediation CD,s, breathe deeply and relax and clear my mind. After completing this daily ritual I explore my goals and see how I am progressing.

This daily focus and clarity around what I want to achieve, helps me to stay on track and ensures that I am taking appropriate action every day to realize my goals.

Meet your Future

This is time you set aside every day to work on your life or on your business. Make a meeting with your future every day. This is time, which is inflexible and nothing should ever get in the way of you conducting this meeting.

Make sure that you have enough time during each meeting with your future, to complete at least five priorities, which are aligned with achieving your goals. This practice ensures that you actually get to make progress towards achieving your goals.

Remember to get your day started with a really nutritious breakfast; this will also help you to stay energized and productive. This combined with your daily success ritual will help you to not only start your day powerfully, but will ensure that you have a really productive day every day.

Your circumstances are unique to you, so it is crucial that you design a daily success routine that suites your individual circumstances.

CHAPTER 18

TAKE CHARGE OF YOUR TIME

Taking charge of your time is easier than you think. If you put any of these ten easy, but powerful, time management tips into action, you'll see an improvement in your productivity. And in your peace of mind.

One: Revamp your self-image: see it and believe it

What's your image of yourself? If it's of someone who's terminally frazzled, that image will affect what you experience throughout the day. To take control of your time, your self-image needs to be of someone who is relaxed and calm and getting everything done.

Close your eyes for a moment. Picture yourself at your best. You're calm and you effortlessly handle whatever challenges come up for you during the day.

You may feel some resistance to this image of yourself. If you do, you need to revise your self-talk. Self-talk is the internal chatter we all carry on within ourselves. Silently say "Let go" to yourself, or "Relax".

The above visualization technique is simple, but very effective. Use it as often as you like during the day.

Two: Make lists

The most effective time managers are the people who use lists the most. When something is on a list, we no longer need to keep it in our mind. The best way to develop the list-making habit is to carry a notebook and pen, or an electronic organizer.

You have a choice of how to make your lists. You can have one enormous list, into which you dump all your tasks, or you can make several lists. Try out both methods, and see how they feel to you.

If you keep an all-in-one list, use a legal pad rather than a small pad, and leave a couple of lines between each task, so that you can add notes. The benefits of using a large pad are that you can add notes and sketches.

Three: Carry a notebook and pen, or an electronic organizer

Carry pen and paper, or an electronic organizer, whichever is easier for you. Some people prefer to use a microcassette recorder and if this is you, be sure than you transcribe your notes at the end of the day, or at the end of each week.

Using a PDA like a Palm Pilot is effective, because you can make notes wherever you happen to be. This means that you can get a head start on some of your work. You can put out the basics of a proposal to a new client over lunch; you can even do it while the meeting is still going on.

Four: Take time out for yourself every day

The time you take for yourself should be spent on doing something solely for yourself. You can listen to music, play a sport, go for a walk, or lie down and take a nap. This is your time to indulge yourself.

Many women interpret the instruction to take time for themselves as a hint that they should spend that time exercising at the gym, or doing something else "worthwhile".

Five: Give the day a mental run-through before you get out of bed in the morning

When you wake up in the morning, think about the day ahead. Imagine everything going smoothly and well. Know that if anything unforeseen comes up, you will handle it. A mental rehearsal sets your attitude for the day. See yourself getting compliments and kudos, so you can start the day with a smile.

Six: Before you start your day, get excited

Enthusiasm is infectious, and so is gloom. Tell yourself you're excited about the day ahead. This might be the day you get a raise: anything could happen. Be determined that something good will happen to you today and nine times out of ten, it will.

Seven: At the end of the day, review and plan for the next day

Take five minutes to go over what you've accomplished at the end of the day. Take another five minutes to rough out a plan for tomorrow.

Eight: Learn to say No

Most of us hate rejecting others. However, you're not doing anyone a favor if you agree to do something, and then do it resentfully. Sometimes we even get in the habit of agreeing to do tasks, and then make excuses. If you know you won't have the time to do a task, don't take the task on.

Nine: Get a routine

Discipline has gone out of fashion. However, the secret to productivity is to have a routine, and to keep to it. If you know that Thursday morning is given over to doing an update on your Web site, you can block out that time each week.

Ten: Don't aim for perfection: just show up

Someone said that 80% of job is just showing up. In other words, just do the job, whatever it is. Unless you're doing surgery, close enough is good enough.

CHAPTER 19

MAXIMIZE YOUR PRODUCTIVITY AND EFFECTIVENESS

Most people walk through life without properly analyzing how they spend their time, money, and energy. That would be fine if they kept quiet and accepted their positions in life. But instead they complain that there just isn't enough time to accomplish everything they want.

Or they complain of not having enough money to buy the things they desire. Or they claim that they have limited energy and get exhausted quickly, and as a result they can't spend leisure time with their family or friends.

Although you may have limited resources of time, money, and energy, you can still use them in the best way possible to achieve what is most important to you in your life.

What you might be missing is the awareness of your daily habits and behaviors that would help you determine how you currently spend these resources.

If you start calculating and keeping records of how you spend your time, money, and energy, you will be shocked by the huge amount of those resources being wasted on activities that are not important at all.

Statistics are not as complex as you might think. In this context, I use the word simply to mean keeping records and monitoring the trends of your daily activities to see how you spend your most valuable resources.

Practically speaking, I strongly advise you to keep LOGS of all your resources. The first should be a time log. For a period of one week, record every single activity you do. It might be difficult at the beginning, but keep it up.

Come on, it's just one week of commitment-and as a result you will experience a dramatic improvement in your productivity and effectiveness. You'll learn a lot about yourself and your behavior. You'll know where your hours go, when they are wasted, and when they are well spent.

Once you have this awareness, it will be possible to allocate and plan your time to perform your most important activities and focus more time on your goals. You'll know exactly how to take control of your time and how to save it for your desired outcomes.

For your personal finances, keep a log of your income and expenses for one month. Record every monetary transaction and, at the end of the month, study the results. You will be surprised. I am sure you'll find some expenses and credit card usage that weren't necessary at all. You'll have a better view on how to use your money more effectively.

You'll have more control over your finances and will be able to save money for what you really want and need. This awareness of where your money goes and where it comes from is essential for better money management and wealth creation. Warren Buffett says that the very first rule of investing is "Don't lose money."

For your energy, keep a one-week log of your energy levels. This concept might be new to you, so let me explain. Every day, keep a log of the hours in which you were fully alert and active and those in which you were lazy or tired.

Draw two lines on a sheet of paper, one vertical and one horizontal. On the horizontal axis, write the hours of the day from the moment you wake up in the morning until you go to sleep at night. On the vertical axis, write the numbers from 0 to 10. These numbers represent your energy level, with 10 meaning fully active and 0 meaning fully exhausted.

Now, for every hour on the horizontal axis (which represents the current hour in your day), put a mark next to the number from 0 to 10 that represents your energy level for that hour. At the end of the day, draw a curve by connecting the points you marked.

This curve will show you your energy level throughout the day. Repeat this process every day so that you can recognize the pattern of your average energy curve. This way you will know your general active hours and lazy hours.

You may ask, "What is the purpose of knowing my energy level curve?" Simply by scheduling your most important tasks of the day- those that need a lot of effort and concentration-during your most active hours, you will become ultra-productive.

Save the easy or unimportant tasks for the lazy hours when your energy and concentration are low. Do you see how this can make you ultra-productive?

How often have you spent your most active moments doing routine or easy tasks, essentially wasting those productive hours on activities that require minimum effort and concentration? And then, when the time comes to do heavy tasks, you find yourself exhausted. That's when you start to procrastinate and perform low-quality work.

I have a friend who works in stationery distribution. Every year he used to purchase a huge stock of stationery and keep it in his inventory. His yearly profits were low, but he settled for them because at least his business was profitable.

One day he decided to hire an accounting firm to record his finances and cash flow and provide a report of his financial position at the end of the year-and that's when he got quite a shock. The accounting firm confirmed that the year had been very profitable.

"Oh, that's good." my friend said. But wait-it wasn't that good. The accounting firm told my friend that he has an excess of money held hostage in the form of unused inventory. Almost 50% of his inventory stock is not used at all.

So, for the next year, they advised him to buy only 50-60% of the amount of stock he used to buy every year. And guess what the result was? That's right-50% of his wasted money in unused inventory will go directly into his profits for the new year.

CHAPTER 20

HABITS TO HELP YOU TAKE CONTROL OF YOUR TIME

Too much to do and not enough time. It's a common complaint among business owners, but it's something within your control. You can actually improve your time management skills with a little discipline and a desire to change.

There's no quick fix or silver bullet to improve your skills overnight. But little changes done consistently will put you on the right path. It's a skill worth perfecting because it delivers some great rewards. More productivity. More time to relax. Less stress from missed deadlines. And when you own a business, more money.

If you want to take control of your time and get more done, then let's create some good habits. By definition, a habit is a behavior or action regularly followed until it becomes almost automatic.

Here are a few that can make a difference when it comes to managing your time.

Goal Setting.

No surprise here. Setting goals and reviewing them daily is one of the best habits you can develop for your business and personal success. Clear goals keep you focused on what's important. They help you prioritize how you spend your time.

Without goals, everything appears important. How will you decide what to work on now, what to work on later or most important, what you shouldn't work on at all?

The key to building goal setting habits is to keep it simple. Write down five or six goals for the coming year. Remember to apply the SMART principle - specific, measurable, accountability, realistic (to you) and time-specific.

Next, for each goal you establish, identify 3-4 things you need to DO to achieve it. Refrain from listing too many tasks or tactics. It makes it easier to focus, take action and stay on track. Goals without action are simply wishes or dreams.

Finally, review your goals daily and use them as you prioritize your days, weeks and months. Invest more time on the activities that move you toward your goals. Learn to ask yourself - Is doing this moving me toward my goals?

Planning with To Do List.

Routine tasks, those you do daily, likely get done without a reminder. You rarely think about them, they are almost automatic. Meetings you schedule are also likely to happen. They are on your calendar (hopefully?).

But what about commitments you make to others? Or unplanned customer or team issues? Or new ideas and strategies for growth that float into your head? Or tasks you identified to support your goals? Or tasks that are important but only need your attention periodically?

As a business owner, you are likely inundated with these things on a daily basis. While most do not require immediate action, they do need action later. So you need to capture them easily in one place - or they will be forgotten (we're human).

Fortunately smart phones are a great tool for creating your to-do list. It's with you most of the time and there are applications to make it easy. While I use Google Task Organizer, Evernote and Wunderlist are also popular apps. Check them out and find one that works for you.

While making a to-do list is important, scheduling time on your calendar to actually work on the tasks is critical. On a weekly basis, review the list and identify the priorities for the coming week. Which tasks do you need to complete or work on? Then block time off on your calendar to work on them.

When it comes to blocking and scheduling your time, keep the following in mind:

View the blocks like appointments - sacred and not to be arbitrarily cancelled. If the tasks are important to you and your business, treat them that way.

Be realistic. Most tasks take longer than we expect and some require smaller blocks over a few days. Don't over-schedule. You'll feel better and stay on track.

People skilled in time management stand to gain more from everyday life. And you can conquer it if you take it one step at a time. Try building these habits into your routine - you'll feel more in control and your productivity will soar.

CHAPTER 21

SUREFIRE WAYS TO BOOST PRODUCTIVITY AND GET RESULTS

We all know that productivity can help us to develop the ways for more wisely spending time in spite of hard times. As a person was productive, he or she could do many things without the direct help of others.

Studies say that to be productive is a very necessary thing in the life of a person since this would help him/her see everything in a positive new way, therefore, it could allow him/her to get through challenges and that he/she has developed manners which could resist the trials and failures.

Top Tips to boost Productivity

For those who just realized how important of productivity is and want to start right now but just do not know how, following are something very useful in this process:

1. You should take your time to re-evaluate and reflect yourself. Almost people think they have already known why they avoid doing self-evaluation. But some studies say they are not able to see that the more they deny themselves of the self-reevaluation, the more they are stuck in their same old routine. This, in fact, leaves them less room for improving.

2. You should list your weaknesses and strengths. If you need developing productivity, it is suggested you should know well your own weaknesses and strengths of yourself. If you already know that then you will know which of your areas to pursue and which of your areas to improve.

After you can identify them all, you will be very easy to set your own goals that are reachable. If you list your own weaknesses and strengths then you will be able to manage, overcome and resolve problems.

3. You should better begin with humble goals. It would be in fact a great help if you avoid putting much pressure on yourself.

And if you just started to boost productivity, you would better start humble so that you would not feel like being defeated if you are not able meet the set goals. If you begin with humble things, you will get greater chances to achieve great future things.

4. You should try to control the progress. You should keep track of how effective of your progress to be productive and that would help you with finding ways that suit best for you.

For the people who just started to develop productivity, it would be great to control how they are progressing so you know which are the areas needed to improve and which are the things you should keep doing.

5. You should share the viral "productivity". Most of people are motivated to continue doing the good things if people around them are happy to follow. In case you are the one that is just beginning to enhancing your productivity, you should find time for sharing and helping others.

And if you think what you are doing is good, it would be great if you can find time for sharing your worthy ideas as well as experience with others so that you can influence them.

People can get engrossed in the details of their lives and chase the next big thing without finding time to complete the projects they previously started. When faced with all of their incomplete projects, they often become overwhelmed and start to procrastinate.

You will find that their productivity decreases and they do not produce the results or environment you are used to seeing. What are the things on your list of things that need to get done?

There are several things that can be done to boost productivity and increase positive results:

1. Capture It. Designate specific times during your day to check email, Facebook, Twitter or any other social media. These can be time wasters, especially when you get into a conversation or await responses.

2. Leave It. Let the voicemail or answering machine take a message when you are working on projects. You can call people back at a time that is convenient for you. Better yet, ask people to leave a good time for you to return their call. Turn off your email notification or "bing" alert.

3. Write It. Keep a notebook and pen handy for those great ideas and the things you need to get done. Writing things down gets the ideas out of your head and onto paper. You will get more done when you see it in the front of you.

4. Do It. Dedicate the beginning of your day to your most dreaded tasks - you know the ones you may have been avoiding. As you accomplish these tasks, you will be motivated to conquer many other things in your day.

5. Recharge It. Take 5 -10 minute mini-breaks throughout your day. Stretch. Go for a walk. Splash cool water on your face. Close your eyes for a moment and do some deep breathing. You will be surprised how refreshed these mini-breaks make you feel so you can challenge the task at hand.

6. Tidy It. Set aside 15 minutes at the end of each day to tidy your desk and prepare for the next day. Make a list of who you will call, email or delegate items to, in order to get your "to-do" list done.

Not only should you see an increase in productivity, but you should get more results - better results. Your motivation and drive will also increase as you reap the rewards of positive results.

CHAPTER 22

KNOW YOUR TRUE SELF AND ACCESS YOUR REAL POWER

If you desire life balance between your inner Self and the outer world, you must practice self-discipline. True power also comes from discipline. It requires that you control your mind and emotions.

It requires that you find ways to honor the inner You. As you practice self-discipline, you gradually develop inner peace. You become more focused and less inclined to waste energy. You get to know your true Self and access your real power.

To know your true Self and reclaim your inner power require emotional discipline. When you feel negative emotion, nip it in the bud. Look instead for a positive aspect. Let go of the common emotions of lack, fear and insecurity.

When you feel overwhelmed with too much to do, pull back and reset your boundaries. Reduce your obligations and eliminate the less important stuff. Choose actions that are more comfortable and reasonable.

Your emotions give you important guidance in making wise choices. They help you know how you are focusing your thoughts. Be aware of your inner critic. Reframe your internal messages as more positive and self-compassionate.

Choose good feeling thoughts. Or at least choose thoughts that make you feel better. With each good feeling thought, you are promoting your well-being and joyful living.

To know your true Self and reclaim your inner power require mental discipline. In your journey from ego to Spirit, you must pay less attention to your intellect and more attention to your feelings.

As you move through the day, ask yourself how each thing feels. If something doesn't feel right, don't proceed. If you feel unsure about what to do, don't act. In the process you cure yourself of the disease of over thinking life. You listen to your inner wisdom. You no longer allow your intellect to dominate your life.

When your mind becomes clear and focused, your emotions feel solid. You grow more self-aware through activities such as yoga, journal writing and gardening. Expressing appreciation often is another powerful way to pay attention to each moment.

You grow to appreciate small things that otherwise go unnoticed. By mindful living you connect with your true Self. You discover your heart's desires. You approach life from a serene, balanced center.

Remember that you are more than your physical self.

To know your true Self and reclaim your inner power require spiritual discipline. Your life is a spiritual journey to remember that you are an infinite Being. There is no one way. But you must have desire and take action. Begin by accepting that you are more than your physical Self.

The Source Energy that creates worlds flows through you. You are an energetic physical being with non-physical roots. You cannot know your Divine Self through intellect and reasoning. But you can have a direct experience of knowing.

By spending quiet time alone, you discover your true Self. Explore meditation as a life practice. It restores the body, calms the mind and empowers the spirit.

You may prefer walks alone in nature or walking meditations. They put you in touch with the rhythms of the Earth. You feel connected to something larger than yourself. You come back in touch with who-you-really-are.

Taking time to nurture the inner You is not being lazy. It allows you to step out of an action-oriented world into a quiet space. You connect with your true Self and align with your real power. You gain clarity of intention and purpose. You return to the world refreshed and ready to share your gifts.

The spiritual journey to know your true Self and access your real power requires discipline. But commitment to self-discipline is just the first step. It helps you stay focused on what matters the most to you. A life vision guides you to live with inner balance and joy.

CHAPTER 23

LIVE WITH FULL SELF-EXPRESSION

The desire for self-expression afflicts people when they feel there is something of themselves which is not getting through to the outside world. ~ Fay Weldon, English author, essayist and playwright

Children have a natural ability to live "out there," fully self-expressed. They're not yet tainted by the heaviness of life, having to do with worrying about what other people think, living up to societal pressures, and fear of retribution. So, consequently, you hear kids saying refreshing things like, "Mom, why don't you stand up to Grandma when she makes you feel bad?"

All they understand is to tell the naked truth. What a free way to live. Of course, we're not talking about the kind of truth that intentionally hurts people's feelings. We're talking about telling people how we feel in a kind way, and not leaving anything important to the well-being of our relationships unsaid.

Speaking your truth by saying what's really on your mind (more on this below) is one way to live more fully self-expressed.

What is Self-Expression?

Self-expression is a display of individuality whether it's through words, clothing, hairstyle, or art forms such as writing and drawing.

Being self-expressed means that people will see your spirit and true character; they will see the totality of who you are. And sharing of one's "self" fully is the ultimate in generosity and is vital for peace, happiness and fulfillment.

Sometimes we are not sure how to access creativity or inspiration, or we know what we want to say or do, but are unsure of how to express ourselves, or feel ill-equipped in our expression of something.

Here are ways to become more fully self-expressed:

Speak Your Truth in the Moment

Did you ever look back on a conversation you had and fantasize about talking to that person in a more authentic way than you did? Perhaps it was someone who mistreated you and instead of telling them how you felt about it, you walked away feeling disempowered and wishing you had stood up for yourself.

For some of us, speaking our truth, in the moment, may be difficult because of fear of confrontation and lack of confidence, but not speaking our truth can have damaging effects on self-esteem and even health.

Start noticing where you may be holding back and when an opportunity comes to speak truthfully (with love and kindness), take it on as a challenge and speak up. With practice, you'll gain more courage and having difficult conversations will come easier.

Widely Define Yourself

"People often say that this person or that person has not yet found himself. But the self is not something that one finds. It is something that one creates," said Psychiatrist Thomas Szasz.

When we think about ourselves, we tend to think in a certain way about our skills, strengths and talents. We narrowly define ourselves, meaning we live life from a certain way of thinking and being, which limits our experiences.

We can re-create ourselves at any time and choose to define ourselves in other ways. Explore new ways of thinking and being, and you may discover that you have talents and passions you never knew existed.

Engage in Creative Techniques

We can help birth ideas and create new possibilities for our life with creative techniques. Through these techniques, we expand our creative aptitude and can potentially achieve a longstanding desire from writing a screenplay to becoming a website designer to making wedding cakes, for example.

Some creative techniques to try include: writing daily about anything that's on your mind, keeping an idea book that you can carry with you, using mind maps for creative problem-solving, brainstorming, and creating vision boards.

Acquire Self Knowledge - Know Who You Are

Many of us rarely, if ever, take time out from our harried schedules to become an observer of our own life and who we are being. We get so bogged down in daily activities and obligations that days, months, and years fly by.

Take time to step back from your life and see whether you are truly happy, fulfilled, using your talents, and pursuing your passions. You can even hire a life coach to help you with self-exploration to gain knowledge that can open up new possibilities for you.

Pursue Wants and Passions Voraciously

Do you feel like something of yourself is not getting through to the outside world? Are you putting your wants and passions on a backburner? This is easy to do with all of our daily responsibilities, but unfulfilled human potential is a tragedy.

Once you have identified who you are and what your passions are, not to pursue them can cause serious regret. Begin now by wholeheartedly committing to your wants and passions. You'll need to set time aside and not let anything get in the way.

Develop a Keen Sense of Reality

Living in reality can be tough, but if we want to become more fully self-expressed we must face and do something about the situations that are not working for us. For example, if we are in meaningless jobs, unsatisfying relationships, or not fulfilling our potential, it's time to honor our truth.

Look at your life and what areas you are not happy with and then work to make positive change. Have faith and trust that things will work out for the better even though, initially, you may be uncomfortable. We have a divine right to be happy and fulfilled and, if we are not, then we have the choice to change.

Full self-expression means to take a leap of faith when necessary, live life to the fullest, make the choices that honor our wants and desires, and not settle for anything less than what we deserve.

CHAPTER 24

THE POWER OF EMOTIONAL SELF-EXPRESSION AND SELF-REFLECTION

The path of self-awareness is not a highway. It is a long, slow process of uncovering and emerging; of discovering and nurturing; of expressing and releasing. In our rush to get where we think we want to get, we forget that our purpose here is to experience the world in human form and then also become aware of our experience.

This is how Infinite Consciousness expands. This is also why we have the inherent drive to express who we are and how we perceive the world. If the need for self-expression gets obstructed or suppressed, a fundamental aspect of ourselves becomes stunted and we suffer as a result: we lose our voice and sense of self.

I am not just talking about expressing our opinions and ideas with others, which involves our logical mind to communicate and does not necessarily require any self-exploration. I am pointing out a much deeper truth about what makes us human: the need to put in words what brews inside as abstract, unclear, and disordered emotional energy.

It is in the expression of our emotional wounds that we can discover and discriminate between who we believe we are and who we truly are: between the conditioned persona who acts and reacts according to an unconscious self-programming, and the sensitive, perceptive, and conscious being that hides behind it and holds all sorts of contradictions, emotions, desires, and aspirations-both positive and negative.

Let Your "Mess" Become Your Message

It takes much courage and determination to look at the aspects that we consider negative, those that made us feel "bad" or ashamed at some point, especially when we were kids, or those that still make us feel inadequate now. These are our "personality flaws" or personal experiences and emotions that we try to hide from others, and most of the time from ourselves as well.

However, they can become our greatest assets when we shift our perspective, and allow our "mess" to become "our message." If we don't give ourselves the opportunity and space to freely express what's been hindering our growth, it remains an amorphous mass of confusing and contradictory energy that maintains us stunted and perpetuates a painful reality

Release Your Internal Critic

We tend to be quite hard and judgmental with ourselves because as we grow up, we create a self-image with an internal critic that conveys the voice of those we have invested with authority-our parents or caretakers, teachers, siblings, and so on.

This is a voice that we have completely internalized, so it sounds as if it were our own and permeates our thoughts. It not only makes us our harshest critics, but it also resonates with anyone we give authority to: our spouses, bosses, partners, opinionated friends, doctors, experts, and anyone who unconsciously reminds us of the authorities from childhood.

This is a voice that disempowers and holds us back every time we want to express who we truly are and how we feel. It stands between us and the world, and redirects the energy of our feelings toward the rational mind, where they get overpowered.

It's the voice of our self-consciousness and low self-esteem. And the more we pay attention to it, the stronger it becomes, to the point where it can completely drown our own. When this happens, we disconnect from our inner compass and lose our footing in the world.

Have you experienced situations where you've felt that what you have shared about yourself was later used against you? Or maybe that it's not even worth trying because it seems that nobody understands what you're saying, as if you were speaking a different language?

Well, the truth is that you are speaking a different language-one that does not match your mental, conscious language because it is a secret emotional language.

This language comes from a wounded place and is non-verbal: it is the emotional energy behind your attitude, your words, your expectations, and your actions. Yet it carries enough energy to drive your internal message and reflect in your reality the wounds that created it, through your relationships and interactions with others.

It comes from the same wounded place that makes you establish relationships with people who are not listening to what you have to say or use your own words to hurt you. It's a language that holds seeds of powerlessness and leaves you feeling small and insignificant.

It's practically like having an invisible sign on your forehead that reads, "I am worthless (disempower me)," "I need to be useful (use me)," "I am insignificant (take me for granted)," or "I am bad (punish me)." You get the idea...

Regain the Power of Your Emotional Self-Expression

This wound-based energy makes you verbal and creative potential lack conviction, clarity, and power because it blocks your true voice, preventing it from coming through and expressing who you are and what you want.

So it's crucial to overturn this energy by letting it out and expressing what it's holding on to-be it fear, shame, guilt, or a distorted self-image. Only then can you utilize it for a more positive, creative, and loving manifestation of life.

I could not stress enough how important verbal expression is for self-growth. I've heard people complain about psychotherapy because they believe it's just a waste of time to talk about your problems, and I agree that it can be on some level if it keeps you on the victim role (and your therapist doesn't kick you out of it),

But once you add the spiritual dimension to what you are drawing into your awareness, the perspective on your behavior and your life experiences changes dramatically because the "victim" quickly dissolves.

It is no coincidence that many cultures have found methods of emotional purification to purge suppressed or hidden emotions-from the Aristotelian catharsis of dramatic identification to the almost mandatory confession of Christianity, or the collective prayer and weeping of death rituals to accept a loss and help bring emotional closure.

They all help us pull back the emotional energy that painful experiences suck out of us.

More importantly, it is the ability to self-reflect and express our perception with words that separates us from all other living creatures and the pack mentality. Words allow us to understand how we feel and how we perceive and create our reality out of the amorphous, disorganized energy that brews inside us.

If simply left to the ruling of the ego-mind, it creates more of the same-old-same that we have been experiencing in our life (and possibly through many lifetimes), but once our awareness takes charge, it becomes the creative fuel with which we can transform our world.

CHAPTER 25

SELF DEVELOPMENT LEADING TO SELF REALIZATION

'Self' means an insight into the psychological personality of a person. A superior thinking about our own self broadens our understanding of attitudes and morals between the actual and idyllic self. This will improve our perspective of analyzing our own self.

Development of self helps an individual to have a deep insight into their inner thoughts. This way he/she can also achieve self-realization.

A person who grows with self-realization knows how to perceive the world around them i.e. their thoughts will be clear on how to carry themselves in the world and stand apart. Moreover, self-development enables the person to carry all the ups and downs of life in a more reasonable manner.

Additionally, if a person will deal with their inner thoughts and actions rationally, they will always have a positive outlook towards life. An entity with an optimistic attitude toward life grows both mentally and spiritually.

Thus, in attaining self-development, one should always concentrate on the development of the mind as well as of soul. It is essential because with more and clearer thoughts, a person's understanding level increases and they automatically inclines towards the state of self-realization.

There are several ways for attaining self-development. Out of which, meditation plays a crucial role in this discovery of one's self-identity. It is a method, which contributes in the outcome of a dignified and blissful state of mind.

This results from the techniques of self-knowledge and self-awareness. It helps us to bridge the gap between individualism and universality. It makes a person selfless and develops spiritually. It makes us think beyond our restricted self. However, before this there is a need to control this restricted self. Meditation serves three main purposes - self-regulation, self-liberation, and self-exploration.

Self-regulation - is a capacity to asses intentionally what we feel and how it affects the functions of our mind and body. Awareness of breath, meditation and relaxation are some of the ways by which this can be achieved.

This helps in reducing pain, nervousness and stress levels of an individual. These techniques come to our aid especially during the situation when we are under constant worry.

It deliberately makes us control this anxiety and helps us relax. For example, if we have indigestion problems while tackling stressful situations, then these techniques can be a way out of the problem.

Self-liberation - meditation can assist us in the attainment of elevated conscious self and recognition of spiritual truths of life. This also gives us support in discovering our own real self that lies hidden behind various personality layers that we have.

These layers keep on adding with our own experience of life. It also develops our faculty of intuition by which we may wonder about certain psychological questions like from where we have come and what lies in store for us in life after death.

Thus, it calls for meditating on our existence as an individual, in relation to society and beyond this world.

Self-exploration - is also one of the most important means of self-development. This involves implication of the meditation techniques of relaxation and concentration. They instruct us ways by which we should apply our attention in the right direction in a calm manner.

These exercises give strength of character and balanced mind. This makes us analyze our virtues and vices. It also makes us recognize the potential that lies hidden within us about which we are completely unaware of.

Along with meditation, techniques of yoga also lend a hand in exploring these potentials from our unconscious. They make our feelings familiar to us and identifying with them. Awareness by widening of our horizons through mental exercises confers a strong on our mind and leads a meaningful life.

CHAPTER 26

THE NEED FOR VALIDATION AND SELF-CONFIDENCE

Self-confidence is above all the belief that you are in control of your present situation in life. It's faith in your ability to be able to cope with whatever may come your way. It's about knowing that your ego is strong enough to remain unscathed by whatever criticism may come your way.

Self-confidence is about the way that you see yourself and not something that is awarded if certain criterions are met. Anyone, regardless of status, appearance, education or background can have self-confidence. It is not something that is gracefully bestowed to a chosen few; it is something that is earned.

It is earned by moving out of the comfort zone and exploring the unfamiliar and the unknown. It is earned by testing our wings where we've never been before. It is earned by exposing our ego and taking the chance to have it bruised.

Self-confidence is the result of a multitude of small victories over inhibition and self-doubts. It's the result of self-examination and self-exploration. It's about testing Nietzsche's famous quote that says, "What does not kill me, makes me stronger."

Bizarre as it may seem, with a poor self-image and little self-confidence, the ego is so fragile that it will view a possible rebuke or criticism as a near life-threatening situation. No wonder it does take courage to expose the self to social situations where the outcome is uncertain.

That's the reason that some people will spend their entire life chained to the restraints imposed by a lack of self-confidence. The fear of being hurt by rejection or some unkind remark is so great that the status quo seems preferable to going through the process essential to break free of those limitations.

A lack of self-confidence is caused by fear. The fear of being ridiculed, the fear of criticism, the fear of failure. In one word, the fear of having the ego bruised. There is only one way of conquering and eliminating a fear and that is by confronting it.

The more a fear is confronted, the more the person becomes desensitized. The more victories over a specific fear, the more confidence grows and the less effective that fear becomes.

Remember the first time you tried to swim underwater. Just sticking your head underwater was a major feat. Two or three days later, you could not even remember being afraid of water. The same principle applies to whatever fear is holding you back from being self-confident.

Most people affected with low self-confidence are under the false impression that self-confidence comes with validation from our peers. They believe that the secret of self-confidence is love and acceptance from others.

Nothing could be further from the truth. Whatever others think of us has absolutely nothing to do with our level of self-confidence. Self-confidence is not the result of validation and acceptance. It's the result of faith in one's ability to be above the ego's petty fears of being bruised or damaged by the opinion or judgment of others.

Having a healthy dose of self-confidence is one of life's most precious possessions. It's the ticket to self-expression and self-actualization. It's not something that will come from the intervention of other people.

It is something that we have to create ourselves. It's done by having the courage to confront our fears by going outside of our comfort zone and doing the things that we are fearful of doing.

The secret of doing this is by starting with small challenges and gradually increase the level of those challenges. There is nothing esoteric about this; it's just applied common sense. Something that anyone can do if the desire is strong enough.

CHAPTER 27

SELF ACTUALIZATION

The term self-actualization has been a subject of various psychological theories concerning individual and individual development. It was originally introduced by a theorist Kurt Goldstein, who described it as a motive to actualize all of one's capacities.

Another theorist, Abraham Maslow, the foremost exponent of the concept of self-actualization described it as an individual's desire for fulfillment, to become what he potentially is or to become everything that one is capable of becoming.

Self-actualization is a being need; and an individual may feel discontent and restless if he is not doing what he is fitted for doing. Self-actualization is an internal force that motivates us to recognize and utilize our abilities and capabilities in order to become what we were meant to become.

It is a continuous process of unfolding our potentials and requires individuals' intensity, direction and persistence of effort towards attaining a goal.

To self-actualize is just like taking some time out of daily life and listening to one's inner self - the subconscious mind (Note: Subconscious mind is a level of mental life existing just below the threshold of consciousness's, where dwells a part of our memory that is accessible by an act of will).

It's like having a direct contact with our soul and asking ourselves questions like: is this what I meant to be, is this what I wanted to be, or is this what I am capable of.

When we actualize our self, we disconnect ourselves from the outside world and shut out the external clues which influence our thinking, feeling and speech; and, go into a vacuum - a space (Note: Space is that area of abstraction, which allows us to comprehend sensual experience.

It is an element of systematic framework that we use to structure our experience': Immanuel Kant in Critique of Pure Reason), which provides us freedom to determine our actions.

As, in our daily life, it is social thought that determines our action. We act as people wants us to act. We become what people want us to become but that is not necessarily what we want to become. And when we are provided freedom to think, we will be able to relate ourselves to our heart and soul and; reason our potentials rationally.

Self-actualization is about living a meaningful life. It's an awakening call persuading us to relate to our inner world and operationalize those latent gifts and talents with which we were born and which we were meant to use and make a difference in life.

However, it is a weak tendency - like a whisper or a quiet voice from within. Therefore it mostly goes unheard. It is to a person to be sensitive to this whispering or quiet voice of the self.

Importance of Self-Actualization

All human beings possess potential to excel. That potential only needs realization and activation to trigger action. Those who do not realize and activate their potentials might go into depression. A person will become a dreamer if he does not put his potentials into practice.

He may feel inspired by his thoughts and potentials but if he doesn't act upon them he will achieve nothing. So, either we realize our potentials and move ahead to lead a purpose full life or else we will cease to exist except as dumb driven cattle and our soul will wither away with time.

Self-actualization evokes a feeling in us that nothing is left wanting, a sense of freedom and liberation, a sense of harmony and satisfaction that, I am an integral part of all that surrounds me and that, I am fulfilling my true individual purpose.

However, it is important to identify toxic actualizations and meanings, and release them from mind as only positive actualization can be useful for oneself and the country.

Self-actualization is not like a seed, which sprouts, in barren soil. It can only work effectively if there is a desire, a will to do so. The socialization from the family - the primary unit, must provide amiable environment to the growth of a broad mind, a positive self-concept and outlook towards life, encouraging an individual to become what he beliefs in.

The realization of one's full potential and setting the same into action is the need of the day. Pakistan doesn't lack in intelligence and talent. Pakistan doesn't lack in resources and potentials. Indeed, our people have proved time and again that they are not incapable of comprehending and achieving objectives.

Such a nation deserves to live with pride and make a contribution to the welfare and progress of the nation. What we lack is probably 'the will' to awake or trigger motivation and this task is as urgent as it is gigantic.

In order to apply and realize what we belief in, we need to continually assess our strengths and weaknesses and count the good things in life.

Being positive and optimistic in approach and knowing that there is always another way of looking at things will make us realistic, logical and spontaneous and we will feel relatively safe, accepted, loved, loving, and alive. We will have a mission in life and lead a meaningful life.

Self-Actualization - Soul Searching - Self-Exploration - Introspection

As already stated above, self-actualization is a tendency to maximize one's talents and potentials. It is a sort of a soul searching that helps us to recognize who we are and who we were meant to be.

Whereas soul searching means examination of one's conscience especially with regard to motives and values Soul searching is a sort of self-exploration, which refers to the examination and analysis of one's own unrealized spiritual or intellectual capacities.

It can be a vision, an intention, a value or an inspiration-anything that helps us in learning, discovering and growing our abilities. The deeper the self-exploration, the closer one comes to self-actualization. Another term, which can be used interchangeably with self-exploration, soul searching and self-actualization, is introspection.

Introspection, according to D. M. Armstrong is a self-scanning process in the brain acquiring information about our current states of mind apt for the production of certain behavior or in short an examination of one's own thoughts and feelings.

Self-actualization is not a new phenomenon. It is not an incorporated foreign doctrine. It is indeed the same khudi (self), about which Iqbal speaks so frequently in his poetry and prose. Iqbal inspired the Muslims with the realization of life and urged them for self-reformation and self-actualization by searching for their self.

He stated that if a person does not take the initiative, if he does not evolve the inner richness of his being, if he ceases to feel the inward push of advancing life, the spirit within him hardens into a stone and he is reduced to the level of dead matter. He wrote:

"Your prayer cannot change the Order of the Universe, But it is possible that praying will alter your being;If there is a revolution in your inner Self, It will not be strange, then, if the whole world changes too". (Iqbal:Zarb-e-Kalim)

Even Quran states that, "Lo. Allah changeth not the condition of a folk until they (first) change that which is in their hearts".

Self-actualization alone can elevate our nation to a progressive level. We have some shining examples of the countries like Japan, South Korea, Greece, Rome, Egypt, before us who overcame social and moral degeneration after realizing their potentials and achieved results that shocked the world.

The Korean nation has gone through tough and harsh times in history and had made quite sacrifices but emerged out more stronger and developed. The underlying fact of their success was that that Korean people always took pride in their country and faced the challenges bravely.

They placed their faith in the hands of able leaders and believed in their potentials and in themselves. The results were astounding; South Korea rose to such a level of economic and technical advancement that it is referred to as the Asian Tiger.

The nation bore the brunt of hard times for a better future. The teachings of Confucius, has a great influence on the thinking of South Koreans even today. The basic ingredients of their remarkable success are hard work, discipline and a sense of integrity and integration arising from patriotism

CHAPTER 28

BECOMING YOUR BEST SELF

There doesn't appear to be anybody or anything in the way to stop you, and yet you just can't seem to take the final leap and get where you want to be.

I've often wondered about this phenomenon and there are probably as many reasons for this as there are people. Fear of failure, fear of success, fear of disappointment, actually, a whole bunch of fears. And when the goal is in sight, you can be pretty sure it's a fear of SOMETHING that stops you from taking those last few steps.

A fear that has come into play several times in my life, surprisingly enough, is the fear of Forever. That is a word that has frightened me more often than I care to admit. There is something so final about forever that it scares the living daylights out of me.

What if I make a wrong choice?

What if I continue to grow and change, and I don't like what I've chosen today?

What if I go this way and miss something incredibly wonderful over that way?

This seems such a silly thing to be afraid of, and yet it can paralyze one for a very long time.

I remember a time when it hit me (the proverbial lightning bolt of understanding) that something that was holding me up from allowing a relationship in my life was the fact that I was committed to self-exploration, growth and development.

I felt that I was constantly changing and was afraid that a relationship that I committed to today wouldn't be the right one in one year, five years, ten years.

One day I was thinking of this and came at it from the other direction. How much was I going to have to change to start wanting a jerk in my life?

Because the qualities I was looking for in a relationship all pointed towards allowing someone in who was basically "nice": loving, supportive, growing, spiritual, etc. And I - finally.-couldn't imagine evolving so much that I was going to stop wanting these particular qualities. In fact, that wouldn't take evolving, but just the opposite.

Recently, I was involved in a workshop on Life Planning. When the leader asked the question "What is stopping you from having the life you want", I was shocked when I realized my uncensored answer was "what if it's the wrong path?".

This is more of that 'forever' thinking. There truly is no such thing as the 'wrong' path. My logical mind knows this: there are no mistakes, there is only experience.

And yet, I was surprised that this fear had resurfaced. Once we have a major realization, we often think that it's behind us, that it won't come up again. Life lessons, however, tend to come at us "onion-fashion". We peel off one layer, work with that a bit, and then one day (sometimes years later) we find the next layer.

So how am I dealing with this Fear of Forever?

I've come up with a phrase that I find helpful, and I have a huge sign on my desktop: "Forever is for as long as it feels right". It may seem silly, but it lets me take a deep breath and put the whole 'forever' thing in perspective. And without doing that, there are some wonderful big steps (like getting married) that I might never have taken.

It is not less of a commitment to the thing that I am choosing. In fact, I think it helps me stay focused in the moment and living in the "now" rather than in the past or future. In reality, all we have is now.

No one can know what the future can bring. That's part of the adventure of life. All I know for sure is that I'm not going to let the fear of forever stop me from delighting in the joy of the present.

CHAPTER 29

THE POWER OF FEELING GOOD ALL THE TIME

Thinking of what you really want is one of the best ways to feel good instantly. Think of what you want and imagine that you are already enjoying it. This way, you are sending a very powerful vibrational frequency to the universe because an emotion such as happiness or excitement is attached to your thoughts.

Another good way to get rid of negative emotions is to do EFT. EFT helps you flush out negative emotions through tapping at certain nerve end points. By doing this, you will be relieved of that unwanted emotion almost instantly. You can check the web out for instructions on how to do EFT if you're not familiar with it.

Another way is to keep your body healthy. In order to do that, of course exercise is a must, but you must also eat healthy foods. And when I say healthy food, what I mean are foods that are as close to nature as possible. Choose organic stuff over canned goods or fruits and vegetables that were bombarded with pesticides and other chemicals.

Stay away from processed foods, fast foods, and foods that contain monosodium glutamate. Things like that are specifically made to weaken your ability to create by disabling your brain to send out vibrational frequencies to the universe.

If you can't send vibrational frequencies to the universe, there is no way that you can manifest whatever you desire. So stay away from those kinds of foods.

The mere thought of what you desire should make you feel better. If you think about what you desire and you feel bad, you must doubt that you're going to have what you want. Belief is also a key factor here. When you believe, you will manifest.

Henry Ford once said that "Whether you think you can't or you think you can, either way you are right." Henry Ford knew the principles and the right process of using the Law of Attraction. That was why he became successful and rich.

When you think of what you want, you know you are feeling good when you feel that it gets you excited and it gets your juices flowing. It is like the feeling when tomorrow is going to be your birthday and you know that you're going to have presents. There is no doubt in your mind because tomorrow is in fact your birthday and for sure, you're going to have presents.

You must feel and think the same way when you want your desires to achieve physical manifestation and become a part of your life. If you want to have what you want there must not be any room for doubt. Only happiness and belief should fill your personality.

As simple as it may seem, this is the real secret. This is the secret that the people who have become successful using the Law of Attraction didn't want you to know about. This is one of the key ingredients in making the Law of Attraction work in your life like magic.

It's like having your own Aladdin's Lamp. You make a wish by simply thinking of your desires, and the universe will put events, circumstances, and people in your life to give you what you want. Think of it most of the time.

And don't forget to feel good whenever you do so. You will then be able to manifest everything and anything you want - in record speed. That's the power of feeling good all the time.

CHAPTER 30

FIGURE OUT THE PASSION WITHIN YOU

What is it that fuels you to be your best, to get up early, to stay up late, to keep on practicing day after day? Is it your family? Is it a desire for a better lifestyle?

Could it be a simple and pure love of playing a particular sport? Do you feel an all-consuming craving from deep inside that you must prove to yourself or someone else you have what it takes to be successful?

What is success to you? What is it you want? Where do you want to be? Who do you want to be?

Is it something materialistic? Is it being the head of a successful business? Does it mean you are truly able to help people, either through inspiration or through financial funding?

If you don't know what your passion is and you're not sure about how to figure out what it is, my hope is that this overview will help you discover what is lying within you that will energize you from this point forward.

Step one, reflect on what it is you really want, who you want to be. Write it down in detail. If this seems challenging, think about what you don't like in your life right now. Maybe the answer lies within the realm of negative motivation. If you are sick and tired of what you've been getting in life, daydream for a while about what you do want.

Think of things that excite you, that make you feel like your endorphins are morphing out and turning into an uncontrollable burning desire. If you can get to this feeling, more than likely you now have a much better understanding of your passion.

Step two is to contemplate on the context of who you want to be. This begins with reflecting on and understanding who you are and what you don't like about it.

What do you want to change the most? This will help you find out what's right, who you really want to be. Envision your ultimate personal character, write down all of the details.

Figure out your specific goals for the next three months, six months and one year. Yep, you guessed it, teacher says "Write them down and prioritize them."

What's the big chip, the one main obstacle you can't seem to let go of that is keeping you mired in the comfort rut of life? Think about the past serious commitments you have made that you never followed through on. What's the commonality, the brick wall you keep running into? Is it a fear? Could it be a lifetime bad habit?

Speak with your mentor about developing a plan of action. If you don't have one, think about people you admire. You may not necessarily have to know them personally. Use your creativity and take the initiative for how to introduce yourself to a leader you admire.

This could be an author of a self-improvement book that has had a solid impact on you. Send them a friend request on Facebook. Reach out to them. Cruise through your cranium, see if you can figure the bigger reasons you might have to take action to achieve your goals.

Being completely honest with yourself, reflect on what level, what type of integrity you want to have with everyone. Who is the single most important person to be in absolute integrity with? Hello? It's YOU. Integrity begins within each of us. If we're out of integrity with ourself, then we're most likely out of integrity with others.

Now you must make sure you focus on every action being geared toward results. This means your focused actions will get you closer to your goals each and every day. This is the basic premise of what is known as the compounding effect. Consistent energy and action gets you closer to your chosen destination.

Work at reaching the point where you can achieving excellence with your day-to-day process. Mindset, organization, self-management, knowledge, and results oriented behavior are all contributing components of your overall soon to be leadership skill-set.

The bottom line is that your results are the only indicator of how you are doing, how you are progressing.

CHAPTER 31

CLARIFY YOUR PURPOSE

Like many of us, we've lost site of what our true purpose is. Without a purpose, it's easy to get side tracked and not really accomplish anything. It's easy to stay at a j.o.b. (just over broke) that we really don't like because we're not focused on our true purpose. So, how do you find your life purpose?

There are several ways. One way is to write down the times that you have felt the most excited, enthusiastic, happy, joyful, and alive. One of the easiest ways to begin clarifying what you truly want is to make a list of 30 things you want to do, 30 things you want to have, and 30 things you want to be before you die."

Everyone has an inner guidance system that tells us if we're "on purpose". When we fill the most joy and happiness, we know we're on the right track. Follow your instincts, and always follow your heart.

Set aside some quiet time and ask yourself:

If I absolutely knew that I would not fail, what would I really like to do?

If money was not an issue at all, what would I like to achieve?

What's really important to me?

What am I passionate about?

What do I like to read and talk about?

What do I desire most?

What really makes me happy?

What activities and hobbies really excite me?

What does success mean to me?

As a child, what did I love to do?

Once you know what your purpose is, organize your life around it. Stay focused, and don't let anything stop you. Read your purpose everyday. Figure out how you can incorporate your passion/purpose into your daily life. Ask someone that has already accomplished what you want to do (find a mentor).

Ask them out to lunch, or ask if you can shadow them for a day. Ask them to share their success stories with you. Most people love to talk about themselves. If, by chance, the person you ask says "no," then you say "next." Successful people are very action oriented. Take action now.

My life purpose is to use my knowledge, passion, and enthusiasm to empower and inspire others to discover their passions, fulfill their dreams, and achieve their life's purpose.

CHAPTER 32

KNOW WHAT ACTUALLY MATTERS IN YOUR LIFE

Given that work is not just an eight-hour disturbance of the day and that you invest many of waking hours on it, it is crucial to begin discovering your passion and real abundant enthusiasm and integrate it in your job.

For you to feel what truly matters it is crucial that you can plainly figure out the how, when, and why of the discovery of discovering pleasure, calmness, and satisfaction in life., if you want to find your passion you should let your heart and real calling guide you.

Or your daily choices at work enable you to be real to yourself?

Have the courage to be true to your enthusiasm and find the job that offers you the chance to do what you want to do in life and live to the maximum. Exactly what are the things that really matter to you at work? Many of these people are experiencing irregular sleeping routines, stress, and left for years wondering what truly matters in their life.

Time is valuable and every day you are asked to make thousands of choices that specifies who you are. Finding the choices that truly matter to you will assist you not to waste your valuable time in life. Know and declare the options that lead you to your enthusiasm."

Ask yourself these concerning questions: "What made your biggest work experience so fantastic? What made your worst experience so bad? What is the most crucial thing missing from your life today?

Follow your heart and dreams and strive on discovering your passion.

"To laugh often and much; to win the respect of smart people and the love of children; to make the gratitude of truthful critics and sustain the betrayal of false pals; to appreciate charm; to find the best in others; to leave the world a bit better, whether by a healthy kid, a garden patch or a redeemed social condition; to know even one life has actually breathed easier due to the fact that you have actually lived."

Considering that work is not just an eight-hour task of the day and you spend most of waking hours on it, it is crucial to start finding your passion and include it in your job. You must allow your heart and real calling guide you if you want to find your passion and purpose and the enthusiasm you need.

Follow your heart and dreams and make every effort on discovering your passion. Finding the options that really matter to you will assist you not to squander your precious time in life.

If you desire to live your life to the max, you need to have the nerve to be real to your enthusiasm and discover the tasks necessary that provides you the opportunity to do it.

CHAPTER 33

KNOW YOUR PERSONALITY TYPE

If you want long-term success, follow your passion. Don't chase the money, the power or the fame - find out what really makes you tick and develop a career or a business based on your passion. I've heard this throughout my life and you probably have heard this too, but then we forget.

When some of our friends and family say, "you need to get a good-paying job", we tend to believe them and fall right back into pursuing a job that will make good money while forgetting all about the things we feel passionate about.

Resist the temptation to take on the belief that your life's work must be hard, boring, and downright painful. There is truth in the advice to follow your passion. If you start a business or a career based on something that excites you, it causes you to jump out of bed in the morning full of ideas and the motivation to work effectively while thoroughly enjoying it.

When you go into business or start a career, you will need momentum and motivation for the long haul and if you are not passionate about what you are doing, that motivation will fizzle bringing you up short of your goals.

As a therapist and a coach, I work with a lot of individuals who have neglected their passions and their authentic self for so long that they don't know how discover what kind of career or business would ignite their fire.

Part of the work we must do, is to identify their personality type so they can begin to get in touch with who they were created to be. In this way, discovering your personality type can actually be an important part of the path back to your authentic self and your passions.

Did you know that you were born with a pre-disposition toward certain personality traits? Just as we are born with a propensity to use our left hand or right hand, we are also born with a propensity to prefer extraversion or introversion, sensing or intuiting, feeling or thinking, and judging or perceiving (as assessed with MBTI®).

Here is an example that might be useful: imagine that there is a little baby who is pre-disposed to preferring introversion (gets re-energized by being alone, needs time to process thoughts and feelings internally before expressing them externally).

This little introversion-preferring baby is born into a primarily extraverted family (extraverts prefer to process thoughts and feelings out loud and feel re-energized by being with people). You can see how this little baby may have to learn how to behave in a more extraverted fashion in order to "fit in" with his extraverted family.

As this child grows into adulthood, he or she may feel different or strange and not understand this "crazy" need for alone time while his/her whole family thrives on being together.

If this child eventually learns that he or she is actually more introverted in nature, then they can embrace that quality and look for ways to work and relate that would appeal more to an introverted type.

Just as a right-handed person will prefer to write with their right hand (even though they are able to use their left hand as well) so also is an introverted person going to function more comfortably and effectively if allowed to use their introversion (even though they are able to use their extraversion when needed).

To sum this up, if you know your unique personality traits (or preferences), you will feel more comfortable working, relating, and functioning within your trait preferences.

If you do not know your unique traits or preferences, you are more likely to think you are somehow different than others and don't know your authentic self as well, since it will not yet be validated in your mind.

As soon as someone becomes aware of their traits and preferences, some of their choices begin to make more sense and they can become much more strategic about how they pursue a career or how they decide to run their own business. T

his is where you are wise to ask for help. If you try to figure out your own traits on your own, chances are you will miss important information that could be vital to your success in life, love and work.

If you are serious about starting a career or business, first know yourself well, then your passions will begin to come to light. There will be more things to consider and more exercises to do to continue to unearth your passions, but simply knowing more about who you were created to be will start this energizing process.

CHAPTER 34

TURN YOUR PASSION INTO THE PERFECT JOB

Unfortunately, most people get so wrapped up in making a good salary they head for whatever job will pay them the most. Sure, they get to provide a comfortable lifestyle for their family, but at what price? Is hating what you do worth making some extra money?

What if you could find the best of both worlds?

Some people fall into the perfect job without any effort - like the guy who takes over the family business. The family business is all he's ever known. He grew up loving it and he's happy being able to carry on the family tradition and stay close to home.

Unfortunately, a situation like that is pretty rare. That's because most people decide to leave the nest and head out to see if the grass really is greener on the other side of the fence. If they find out it isn't, they feel "stuck" in a job they hate.

Luckily, though, these decisions aren't permanent. No matter how old you are - or no matter how long you've been working in your current profession - it's never too late to create a new career path based on your passions. If you think there's no money in that, think again. As soon as you understand your passions, you'll discover there's a big world out there.

Here's what you need to do:

Take a step back and examine where you are and how you got there. Figure out exactly what makes you unhappy about your current situation. Even though it's your life and decisions you've made, you'll probably be amazed when you sit down and carefully think about it all. The blur of the past 5 or 10 years will come into focus and you'll start to really learn about yourself.

Think about what you're passionate about. How can you incorporate them into a career? To do this, you'll have to be creative and look at your passions from a variety of angles.

For example, if you love to travel, why? Does your passion stem from seeing new places? Meeting new people? If you simply enjoy meeting people from all walks of life, look for a job that allows you to do just that.

Learn everything you can about your passion. Even if you love it, you may not know all there is to know about it. Maybe there's an angle you haven't thought of yet you can turn into a business opportunity.

Don't confuse your passion for admiration. Just because you admire the great book you just read doesn't mean you have a passion for sitting down at your computer and working as a writer.

Remember that everything takes time. The people who are making a good living off of their passions didn't get there overnight. You generally don't get to start out doing something you love and making a ton of money. However, if you're really passionate about it, you'll enjoy climbing the ladder and gradually seeing more success.

No matter where your passions take you or what your bank account looks like at the end of the day - you owe it to yourself to get out of your current rut and try something new. Even if it doesn't work out the way you originally planned, you'll have fun on the ride.

CHAPTER 35

ACCEPT THE GIFT OF YOUR OWN RESPONSIBILITY

Remember when you were a kid, the dreams you had, how you were going to live life on your terms? You weren't going to be like your parents, old and boring. You and your friends had big plans. "Not me", you all claimed, "My life's going to be different". None of you could articulate what 'different' meant but you knew you wanted more than the adults around you.

Of course, you were either humored, put down, gently, harshly or worse, ignored with the standard "What do you know about life anyway? You're just a kid." In a blink, you're in college (maybe) or already stuck at eighteen living a life you abhor.

Feeling lost and depressed at fifty you ruminate on your dreams back then. You were chomping at the bit to 'get out'. One or three of your friends made it but not you and so, you wonder what went wrong? How did you lose yourself and end up this treadmill to nowhere?

You hate your life, your boss, job, co-workers, and the daily commute, constantly throwing proverbial rocks at everything. It changes nothing but you continue anyway.The fact is that what you resist persists.

The more you detest something, the more dominant it becomes in your life. When you feel so passionately about anything you dislike you reinforce that resistance.

I've never heard a bird half-sing, a hawk half-cry. When ready, speak your truth with conviction. To end this stuckness and recapture your dreams:

Accept the gift of your own responsibility.

Be mindful of your thoughts.

Speak your truth quietly and clearly.

Identify your passion and recapture your dreams.

Leave home?

Chronicle your growth.

1. ACCEPT THE GIFT OF YOUR OWN RESPONSIBILITY

If you desire positive, lasting change in your life that makes you feel fulfilled, take responsibility for your own life. It's your gift to yourself and it's precious.

Accept situations exactly as they are. When you do, your reality changes and you begin to see things as they really are. Fighting against what is is futile. and that simply reinforces your frustration and negativity.

It is important to understand that it's your interpretation of what someone said or did that creates our angst. Drop the story. End it or take action and move on. Just stop regurgitating it in your head.

Acknowledge the part you played that has brought you to your current feeling of stuckness. Start from exactly where you are. Express your dissatisfaction and longing to those who matter then go find your passion and recapture your dreams.

No excuses, no apologies. If you intend to live life on your own terms, accept responsibility for how you feel, what you think, say and do. Nobody on this planet can make you feel happy, sad, bad or mad. It's all up to you. Your power is internal and that's where change takes place.

2. BE MINDFUL OF YOUR THOUGHTS

Change begins with being mindful of your thoughts. Your initial awareness creates an internal shift which expands as you progress. You have no doubt heard that Insanity means doing the same thing over and over again yet expecting a different result. That's the problem right there. Nothing will change until you do something differently.

Question every thought and ask yourself, "Is that true?, Do I really believe that? Who taught me that? Where/how did I learn that?", "Does that even make sense anymore?"

Discard those beliefs as needed (it becomes easier over time) and replace them with uplifting ones.

It takes thirty days to create a new habit. Vibe with what's true for the new you. The old you did its job by bringing you to this point. It's time to start accepting yourself exactly as you are including those characteristics and body parts you dislike.

Stop beating yourself up and begin loving yourself. Show up in your life by being real. You answer to no one but yourself.

It's not an easy task as we're all accustomed to acting as automatons based on what we learnt at our parents' knees. You'll forget to "check in" sometimes, however, with practice it improves and you'll gain more insight into your actions.

3. SPEAK YOUR TRUTH QUIETLY AND CLEARLY

It's not rocket science to end displeasing encounters. Decide to separate yourself from the herd to avoid being stampeded over an emotional cliff in a knee-jerk reaction whenever someone pushes your buttons. Take deliberate action to end many unpleasant situations in your life and stop re-acting.

You ought to know by now what triggers you. Be prepared to handle them differently when they occur. No more playing small. Whatever displeases or angers you is an issue to be resolved and released as anger is repressed passion.

The fact is that those around you mirror back at you what you think and feel about yourself. If that wasn't the case, you wouldn't react. Express yourself.

Quietly speaking your truth takes courage (with a corresponding loosening of tension) but only because you're unaccustomed doing so. That's your gift to yourself. By acting out of the norm, your interlocutors are stopped in their tracks.

Some will continue their antics but will be unable to antagonize you. Understand that people only discomfort you when you already feel uncomfortable about a particular subject matter.

Have the courage to meet people half-way, admit when you're wrong, apologize, agree to disagree, concede a point made, back down (life is not a contest and you don't have to win every time), smile, don't speak and walk away, show people the respect they deserve, stand in your truth, and most importantly, draw the line. In the latter case, being real is essential. Be fiery if need be..

Stop allowing other people to dilute or poison your day with their words or opinions. Stand strong in the truth of your beauty and journey through your day without attachment to the validation of others. Dr

4. IDENTIFY YOUR PASSION AND RECAPTURE YOUR DREAMS

Become the observer in your life. Ask yourself the following questions to begin the process of identifying where your life went off-course. The responses will be enlightening.

What happened to make me give up my dreams?

What did I do today that I could have had a different result?

When did I start depending on others to tell me what to do?

When did I stop acting of my own accord?

When did I stop saying what I wanted?

Why did I decide to give away my power?

To recapture your dreams and identify your passion after a long hiatus start with the Internet. It's a treasure trove of information. Connect with people in your community and also those involved in the area that interests you.

Seek out friends, entrepreneurs and anyone else whom you believe would be able to provide more information to take you on your chosen path.

Your actions and new way of being will have an impact on those who know you as you follow your new path. Unless someone is on your wavelength and supports your dreams, desires and goals, keep them secret until you encounter those who support you.

Until then, nurture them in your secret garden with abundant flows of imagination, grow them with goals, flesh them out with plans, and take action to bring them to fruition. Every action counts no matter how small.

Nothing and no one is off-limits. You won't get a hearing if you continue to place safe. Risk means stepping out of your comfort zone. How will you get what you want if you don't ask for it?

Joy naturally results when you pursue your dreams. You're passionate. Your enjoyment, fulfillment and satisfaction of the life you chose is thus assured. That burning desire keeps you enlivened and enthusiastic in everything you do. Dreaming big is the only way to go.

When you lack passion joy is absent on achieving a goal or dream. Your satisfaction is fleeting and feels unsatisfactory producing a prosaic "okay, now what?" response and this cycle continues until you tap into what's really important to you. Many are still toiling uselessly and mind-numbingly in that barren vineyard they call life.

More people are waking up in their unfulfilled lives shaken out of their torpor by a crisis of some sort (health, near death experience, bankruptcy, emotional breakdown or other major life event) that forces them to take stock.

When your chosen work is your passion it's no longer just a j.o.b. Despite the requisite challenges you love going to work every day. You're on fire with a let's do this attitude.

The time for playing small has passed. In fact, it led you down the garden path. Be selfish. Demand what you want and say how you want it. Go where you will find it. Release the old you. There's no going back.

If you can't figure out your purpose, figure out your passion. For your passion will lead you right into your purpose. Bishop T.D. Jakes

There's no such thing as failure. A lot of "no's" will come your way but so what. All you need is the first "yes". Lack of success tells you to go back, review and modify. If you listen to the naysayers you'll end up right back where you started, with them.

Synchronicities and coincidences tell you when you have struck gold. That means you're in alignment with your cherished dreams, desires and goals. Don't stop now.

5. LEAVE HOME

The beauty of this work is that it doesn't necessarily involve leaving home, family or friends. But it might. Leaving precipitously will be counter-productive. As I well know, you can't escape yourself. Wherever you go, there you are so take care of business now because you'll never pass this way again.

Refuse to feel constrained by your present circumstances. From the moment you decide to stand in your truth despite nervous butterflies, you immediately change the outcome and reinforce your power every time you speak up. You will begin to see and feel tangible, positive results in all that you do.

None of this means that your emotions have vanished. You're human after all. However, you're now aware of them and they're under your control. They no longer control you and when they do that'll be your choice.

Remember, no one can make you feel happy, sad, mad, or bad. That's giving away your power which is internal. Depending on external forces to dictate your actions or believing that someone makes you feel a particular way negates it away.

6. CHRONICLE YOUR GROWTH

Mark the date in your diary when you decided to identify your passion and recapture your dreams. Maintain it for one year to chronicle your growth.

Review your diary one year later and be amazed at the changes in your life, of how much you've grown simply because you decided to become present in your life, you stood your ground and spoke your truth quietly and clearly.

Start a gratitude journal and list five to ten things that you feel grateful for every day, no repetition. I guarantee it won't be a chore or a bore. Become one of the minority on the planet who look forward to going to work to do the job they love with a passion, every single day, and get paid for it. That puts you on a natural high and gratitude is a logical outcome.

Meditate every morning before getting out of bed to center yourself, tap into your power and plan your day. Always, do the most important task first, every single day and you'll see a significant difference in your output. Also meditate at night before going to sleep. It's a perfect recipe for a restful night.

You control your thoughts. You decide what to think and do. You live your life either in joy, sorrow or regret. It's your choice.

CHAPTER 36

DISCOVER WHAT YOU SHOULD DO WITH YOUR LIFE

A Calling is an individual's highest purpose. Everyone has this kind of purpose or calling in life. And everyone has also been generously endowed with the talent necessary to fulfill it. The value of a calling is on two levels. First, it is the means to an individual's greatest possible growth, success, and happiness.

And second, it is the avenue through which one makes the greatest contribution to the world. But there is one characteristic of a calling that is particularly cherished by those of the Lazy Persuasion. A calling is, by marvelous happenstance, the easiest, most irresistible path to follow, the easiest path that produces the most results.

Once you choose to stop denying what makes you happy, your life naturally evolves. All the signs are there, do not ignore the obvious. When you make a true decision to let yourself be directed by your natural enthusiasm, it gives you clarity. What you do isn't work but a lifestyle.

Go for what expresses you and completes you. It gives you a sense of connectedness to your past and ties your life together. You can get good at what you need to serve what you believe in. The true search is for what you believe in. The difference is whether your heart is in it.

Your life does not work when you oppose your soul's nature. If you want a magical life, you have to drop your inauthentic transactions with the world.

You discover your own power when you spend time alone to figure out what you really love to do. Life is nothing but a hollow sham without passion. The world needs you to be an enlightened giver of your dream.

What do people really want?

The want to find work they are passionate about. Productivity explodes when people love what they do. We are not looking for fulfillment as we are already full. We are looking for work that gives us opportunities to give our true gifts. It is something we find ourselves drawn to, something we want to make happen. Something we believe as the ideal.

Individual success will not be attained by migrating to a particular "hot" industry. Individuals that thrive will do so because they focused on the question of who they really are, and from that found work they truly love, and in so doing unleashed a creative power they never imagined.

The vocation that you are in will result in the kind of subjects that will occupy your mind daily. Choose the vocation which resulting thoughts are what you would want to occupy your mind with.

Do not make the mistake of doing something that causes you to think about things you'll find boring and not so meaningful if you have to think about them all the time. The things that you think about the most throughout the day really become what you are.

You must focus on a specific target market that you love and want to work with for life. This makes it easy for you to stay motivated, it brings you more fulfillments in life, and it lets you make a very nice living in the process.

Target a market that you would love to work with, even if you didn't get paid for it. Pick a group of people you can relate to. Picking a market you are suited to exploit first, then going after saleable products is a smart approach.

Money is made so that you can use it to fulfill your vision. Doing something that makes you money as the sole reason without the purpose of creating something bigger is quite meaningless.

Choose to be involved in a field where you can learn the most in every area that advances your personal development and dream while building your career/business simultaneously. The best way is to do something that makes you money as well as help you in fulfilling a big vision that you have at the same time.

It is fine to have financial goals as long as we understand that we use those finances to helps us live the live we deserve while at the same times allowing us to fulfill our mission.

We don't experience fulfillment as a result of "having more." We experience fulfillment by fulfilling our life's purpose. By expressing our talents and gifts and by sharing them with the rest of the world.

You should be engaged in a business that you love and furthering movements with which you are in sympathy. You will then only do your best work and take intense pleasure in your business. In this way, while constantly growing and developing your powers, you are at the same time rendering through your work, genuine and devoted service to humanity.

No one is naturally lazy. You are naturally productive where your passion lies. But first you have to find your passion that is the key. Many people are passionate, but because of their limiting beliefs about who they are and what they can do, they never take the actions that could make their dream a reality. -Tony Robbins

Usually all we get at first is a glimmer. A story we read or someone we briefly met. A curiosity. A meek voice inside, whispering. When we choose to observe and explore it, the rest will start unfolding. The rewards of pursuing it are only for those who are willing to listen attentively, only for those people who really care.

A calling may not be something you consciously realize early in life. It's something you grow into, through trials and mistakes. Freedom is the confidence that you can live within the means of something you're passionate about. Failure's hard but success at the wrong thing can lock you in forever.

Business is a tool to support what you believe in. Our calling is a vehicle to let our real selves out. Work is an expression of life.

It is certain that you can do what you want to do. The desire to do it is proof that you have within you the power which can do it. Desire is power seeking to manifest. Deep down inside you know you can do it, that's why you want to do it. Every desire is possibility seeking expression through life.

The desire to play music is the power which can play music seeking expression and development. The desire to speak before millions is the power which can inspire the world seeking expression and development. The key is development.

When there is no power, either developed or undeveloped to do a thing, there is never any desire to do that thing. When there is strong desire to do a thing, it is certain proof that the power to do it is strong.

The more unbreakable a desire is, the more unbreakable the power present is. Within your passion is genius. Power comes from purpose. It is God that works in us both to will and to do.

Being abundant is your birthright. It is a lot easier to succeed than it is to fail, you have to work hard to fail, whereas to succeed you only have to let go. If you knew how much energy you invest in creating failure you would drop it in an instant.

When you resist abundance, you are going against your natural state. For example, resisting a desire to become an artist or make that phone call, or follow a childhood dream are all ways in which we resist. We are literally cutting off our energy flow. Being untrue to ourselves makes us unfulfilled.

You can learn to follow through on those activities that you love and give you a feeling of being open and energized. Just remember doing what you love will open up your energy, and opening up your energy will allow abundance to come into your life.

We are not here simply to "help others", we are here to LIVE, and to do whatever expresses our joy. This might INVOLVE helping others, but only if it brings you joy to do so.

(Do not get the conceptual focus of expressing joy confused with the infinite number of ways that joy can be expressed in physical reality, or you're simply adding another rule to how you can express your love and joy.)

Self honesty is important in this area, because we often like to adopt a sense of false humility about such things, believing that we are "spiritual" from doing them, rather than just from being who we are.

Most people spend the majority of their life trying to figure out what is it they came here to do. And the majority of them come to that realization at the end of their lives. Why?

Because right before they are about to make their transition, they realize that the work they came here to do had nothing to do with figuring things out. It had to do with doing the things that brings them joy. So the work we came here to do has nothing to do with figuring anything out.

It is something that arises naturally as a result of doing the things that brings us joy. When we do so, something magical takes place. We find ourselves in careers we never even thought of being a part of.

Joy is your inner guide. You will always feel happy when you do what's right and not what you think is right. Joy is the measure of being authentic. When you follow joy, you will always feel peace. Joy and peace are one.

Do not create a dream to be trapped by it. A dream is meant for you to express yourself in freedom. Do not set goals which don't leave you any freedom to maneuver.

Your innermost desires are divinely inspired. When you feel passionate and excited about something, it is God's way of telling you that this is your purpose and mission in life. Your passions are God's way of leading you.

Every positive thought, idea an inspiration you have is a message from God. God is the universal mind who communicates through your mind. His message comes through your feelings, intuition and thoughts. God leads you from within.

By choosing to follow your heart, you are fulfilling what God has placed in you. Your calling will become more clear to you when you reach a point in life where all your past experiences have a connection that points you in a certain direction of possibility.

Following your calling puts you in the path where God's blessings for you are pouring. As long as you are moving in the direction of your life's purpose, watch the universe bless you with all the things you need in order to fulfill your dreams.

You will find many precious and priceless things in the act of walking your life path. Everything that you need to experience abundant life to the fullest will come to you through following your calling.

CHAPTER 37

CREATE ABUNDANCE THROUGH JOY

To discover your life's vocation is to observe what you most love to do, what you seem to want to do naturally and what skills you've learned along the way. When you love what you do and you're doing what you love time goes by unnoticed; you feel fulfilled.

When you are fulfilled, nothing else matters; making money doing it is immaterial to you because the driving force is joy, not money. In this state of being, you radiate joy and therefore, by the Law of Attraction, only more joy can come to you.

So the question becomes, when you let go of your (and everyone else's) preconceived notions about who and what you should be, what are you automatically drawn to? What skills do you enjoy using?

When you release what feels like effort and choose to focus only on what brings true joy to your heart, your life's work will evolve from that joy coupled with the use of your natural and learned skills.

Sometimes we have a limited perspective of what one could consider a "skill" and that can interfere with our ability to see our own gifts. Skills are not necessarily visually obvious...such as being a great artist or designing magnificent buildings. Skills are not necessarily audible such as being a musician or a great orator.

Your skill and joy can come from something as simple as being an uplifter to those with whom you come in contact. Perhaps you enjoy creating beautiful environments or working with plants.

Perhaps you like sewing or making little ornaments out of unusual pieces of wood. It doesn't matter if the world would define your skill as grand. It's how it makes you feel inside that is important.

I know of a man named Colonel Sanders whose skill was hidden in a chicken recipe he had. He totally believed in the magnificence of his recipe. One day it occurred to him that others might like it as well, that perhaps he could sell it and make money. Thus Kentucky Fried Chicken was born.

Initially I had trouble identifying my passion because, "I didn't have a passion. All I wanted to do was study the higher mind teachings and figure out how to apply those to daily living."

I didn't realize that this was my passion that my niche was in my inherent ability to see the latent potential in those who aspired to know their authentic selves and to help them manifest this potential on earth.

The passion was so close to my heart that I was blind to it, thinking I had to take up music or art of some sort when all I really wanted to do was find the God-Self within.

So where is your passion hiding? Start by identifying that which brings you joy. What would you do if you didn't have to worry about money or other restrictions or obligations? Here we find the direction of your soul's work.

You don't have to have a business proforma ready to produce to the world just yet. Just enjoy being in your joy. Then concentrate on using the special skills you have acquired along the way and appreciate that you have them.

Attend to them. Make them bigger. Make the joy bigger. See how you can use those skills in other areas of your life so that you are turning all your activities into expressions of your life's work. This will begin the process of drawing opportunities to you for making money and supporting yourself.

As always, whenever you're feeling great about what you are doing, make the "greatness" bigger. Visualize yourself becoming aware of ideas as they come to you.

See yourself ready to take action when opportunity presents itself. See yourself being supported by the universe for your endeavors; making money easily and effortlessly as ideas begin to take shape.

Create these pictures first; building an etheric prototype of your ideal and allowing it to morph into "the perfect idea". This will also take some of the angst out of trying too hard to hear a nebulous voice inside of you; making you more and more receptive to the plan that your soul is emitting to you.

Allow your inner creativity to expand your concepts about what is possible and worry not about whether you have all the required skills to create it. Opportunities for further development will flow to you naturally as "next steps" as you live into your dream.

Stretch your imagination, and your ability to manifest will develop as well. By milking the joy of your personal expression, by making it grand and seeing it as the seed for bringing value into the world; by appreciating the skills and talents that you already possess; by going beyond what you think is possible, you will find the key that opens the doorway to your unlimited potential.

CHAPTER 38

LEARN TO MANAGE THE GAP

SWhen it comes to achievement, much of the success research highlights that there is an inner and outer game. Most people make the mistake of focusing solely on their outer game, the elements of engagement that others can see.

However, it is through the mastery of the inner game that we truly begin to enjoy and experience the level of success that we are truly capable of. The biggest element of our inner game, and therefore a key success factor, is how well we Manage the 'Gap'.

When a stimulus is applied we have built-in responses to it, responses that we have conditioned over time, similar to Pavlov's dogs salivating at the sound of a bell.

Someone makes a derogatory comment about how we look in our outfit and we get upset

A co-worker doesn't agree with an idea we brought forth and we get angry

Someone cancels dinner with us and we get depressed

Someone cuts us off on the highway and we feel rage

All of these may be automatic responses, operating unconsciously, but they exist because at some point in our past we set them up to be our preferred response to that stimulus. Good news though, we can condition a new response.

Despite the fact that it feels like a direct and instantaneous route from the stimulus to our response (feelings) there is actually a gap in there, providing us with the opportunity to assess the stimuli and determine our responses.

Most of the time we simply opt for easy and therefore siphon the response off to our conditioned default setting. But we can break this pattern if the result is not desirable. There are three key steps to creating the right foundation for the shift to occur.

Begin by determining that the existing behavior is undesirable. You have to want to change it more than you want to keep it. If you 'like' feeling depressed, angry or hurt you will not be able to let the behavior go until you paint yourself a picture of the new behavior that is more positive and serves you more.

Although it may not make conscious sense that we would prefer a negative result over a positive one, people hang onto negative outcomes all the time. If we hold a negative view of ourselves then we will seek out supporting negative outcomes.

We have to consciously determine that we no longer want to feel bad, be overweight or unhealthy, lack the income or success we desire for us to be able to move in a different direction.

You have to believe that it is your job to change it. Not some higher power, not your mother, not your boss, not your spouse, not the guy next door. It's your life, your behavior and your responsibility.

If you defer this to someone else then you will simply wait for them to 'fix' it for you, which isn't going to happen. Only you can fix it, but you have to take responsibility for it to happen.

You have to believe that you can. You must believe that it is within you to control your responses and change it. If you believe that you are at the mercy of that conditioned response

(I call this the Popeye Principle: I am what I am and that's all that I am) then... you're done. You have to believe you have all of the requisite knowledge, skills, ability and desire to make it happen.

Master these three steps and you are on your way to living a life of your choosing and enjoying the outcomes your most desire. Managing the Gap is not always difficult, but it is necessary if you want to change your responses and results.

It doesn't even matter if you 'see' a gap or not. Trust that it's there, believe the change is within your control and step into the new behavior/response.

CHAPTER 39

ATTITUDE CREATES YOUR ALTITUDE

If you want to elevate your life, you must look at your attitude first. Attitude is the number one secret of success. Read on if you're ready to climb to new heights today.

Your attitude shapes every single day. Each one of us has incorporated beliefs and "truths" about life into our daily thoughts. These thoughts lead to action, which then creates results.

If you're not happy with the results you're getting in life, then you need to seriously evaluate your attitude. Often the beliefs we consider to be "truths" are nothing more than fabrications of our subconscious.

What problems do you face day in and day out? It's likely that whatever "eats" at you on a daily basis is your beliefs, thoughts and feelings surrounding these issues. Write these problems down and then evaluate your thoughts about them.

For example, if a lack of money is a constant issue, consider carefully your beliefs about money (and write them down on paper).

Do you find yourself resenting rich people?

Do you consider rich people to be thieves?

Do you feel that rich people are snobs and poor people and the middle class are honest, kind-hearted folks?

Do you feel you'd make more money if your boss was a nicer person, or didn't "have it in for you?"

Do you believe less qualified workers get the promotions you should be getting because they "suck up to the boss?"

All of these beliefs and thoughts amount to nothing more than your subconscious feeding your mind with mistruths, falsehoods and justifications, just so you can feel better yourself and your current state of affairs.

More specifically, your subconscious places these ideas in your mind so you can feel good about not taking any action to improve your situation.

It's easier to be angry at those more successful than it is for you to take the steps to gain your own financial security and freedom. Worse yet, those thoughts create even more pessimism, cynicism, anger and resentment which places you in a constant cycle of doing nothing but stew in a bath of unproductive, stress-inducing thoughts.

In other words, your beliefs about money (or the lack thereof) lead to action (doing nothing) which results in getting nowhere on a daily basis.

Can you see now how your attitude affects the outcomes you realize each day? It doesn't matter what problems you face - money, relationships, career - your attitude will be the key in resolving or perpetuating these issues.

The great news is you can change your attitude immediately. It does not own you. You are its master, but only if you choose to be. How do you "feel" about making today different than yesterday? It's entirely up to you.

CHAPTER 40

TAKE BACK LOST CONTROL

The only way you can be successful in life is if you become the absolute master of your destiny. For most people, this is usually not true simply because as they grow up, they lose control of one of the most important keys to success.

Without the ability to control your mind, there is really no way that you can be certain of success. It is that simple because it is the mind that controls every aspect of our lives from our attitudes to our emotions. One of the most important parts of the mind is the subconscious mind.

This is so simply because it is the part of the mind that shapes our experiences and determines how we respond to them. However, unlike the conscious mind which we are in total control of, we never are usually aware of how this part of the mind is influenced and when it actually influences our actions and reactions.

Since most people usually leave the influencing of the subconscious mind to the external environment and society in general, they are usually not in control of their minds.

As a result, they usually leave their destinies to be at the mercy of society and in the end, they end up being victims of circumstances and "life" in general. Without absolute control of their minds, they lose sight of one of the most important secrets to success.

The key to success in life lies in your ability to control your mind. The more control that you have over your mind, the higher will the chances of you being a success in life become. This is so simply because it is the mind that is at the center of all the activity in our lives. We literally do nothing without engaging our minds.

While most people are usually aware of the power of the conscious mind, they are rarely aware of the power of the subconscious mind. In fact, they are usually ignorant of the most important part of their minds.

This is so because the sphere of influence of the subconscious mind usually extends to the conscious mind. It therefore also influences our thinking and decision making patterns and as a result, it is usually to blame not only for our successes as human beings, but also for our failures.

Given the magnitude of power that the subconscious mind has over our lives and thus over our destinies, it is important that we learn how to control it. Learning how to do this is the secret to taking total control of our destinies. It is the only key to success that can guarantee success in life and in business.

CHAPTER 41

THE SECRETS OF MANIFESTATION

Much has been said about the importance of visualizing our dreams in our minds for us to be able to realize it, but the complex process that details how exactly it can be done is rarely being discussed.

You need to decide on what goal you would be after, meditate and immerse your mind with optimism and positive thoughts, and wait for the universe to magically align with your plans.

Although this is not necessarily a bad thing, it is still lacking and incomplete and would therefore result to an utter waste of time and effort. The Secrets of Manifestation tell us about the missing steps in the pattern to fully maximize the efficiency of this pattern in order for us to succeed in life.

One of the most vital, and yet one of the hardest to master as a habit to become a confident and successful person, is the trait of being passionate and wholly committed to one's ambitions. Your own goals should be your own motivation and source of inspiration.

If you desire something so passionately and intensely, you are not only sending out a message of affirmation of your intentions, but you are ultimately sealing it with utter confidence and steadfastness. This is one of the core foundations of fully maximizing the potential of the secrets of manifestation in your life and career.

Perhaps if we evaluate our lives, one of the most strikingly similar things that all of us could agree on is the difficulty of the inner inconsistencies in our lives. Most of the time, this is the exact same reason that stands between us and the dreams we want to achieve.

We are very much aware and committed to our conscious desires; wants and needs but we often neglect to pay particular attention to what our subconscious intentions are, thereby creating a conflict that is most of the time unbeknownst to us.

The secret of manifestation is to unite these two differences and remove any sort of confusion that will inevitably hinder the success you are aiming at.

When it comes to living our lives, we can only be either one of the two kinds of people: one whose main goal is to win, or one whose objective is not to lose. At the surface they might be two similar things, but there's a huge gap of contrast between them.

The secret of manifestation is to know the difference and to decide which among the two classifications you would want yourself to fall under. You can either be the passive one that takes comfort in convenience and a life of minimal risks, or you could be someone who is all set to play aggressively in order to get what you want in life.

It's a simple choice, and the choice is always yours. The universe we live in is the continual provider of abundance and prosperity, once you apply and master the secrets of manifestation your plans, needs and desires will consistently and unfailingly be met.

There are secrets to be discovered that can ensure you will attain everything you desire in life. A life filled with riches, abundance, happiness and health can be all yours.

CHAPTER 42

DEMONSTRATE ATTRIBUTES AND ACTIONS FOR SUCCESS

Before applying the secrets of success, one must understand what they are. This chapter purpose is to demonstrate how the secrets of success are applicable to any of our goals, pursuits, and dreams in life. Below I have listed the secrets of success:

Put God & Family First

Desire Success

Dream Big, Think Big, & Think Differently

Believe in Yourself & Believe Your Dreams Are Possible

Eliminate the Voices of Fear & Doubt... Continually

Completely Commit & Be Totally Determined

Establish an Organized Plan & Goals

Take Action Now & Work Hard

Learn From & Get Up After Failures

Persist Always & Never Quit

These principles are the requirements, attributes, and actions necessary in order to accomplish success in life. They apply to any situation, and to every individual.

However, learning about and understanding these secrets is relatively simple; the difficulty is implementing them. And yet, when they are understood and applied, they literally are the formula to accomplish any of our goals, pursuits, or dreams.

Below I have listed several goals, situations, and pursuits from various categories and areas of life that are applicable to everyone. As you will see, your potential and success in any endeavor is determined by you alone.

The realization of your goals is not solely determined by circumstance or location, ability or knowledge, money or family heritage, others, or even race or gender.

The secrets of success are attributes and actions that can be learned and implemented by everyone and are applicable to any goal or pursuit; thus, you literally can become and accomplish anything in life - it is up to you.

1) Eat Healthy & Exercise: How much longer will we as a culture continue to believe that the latest diet, surgery, gym membership, or pill is the solution to our poor nutritional choices and lack of exercise routine?

Eating healthy and exercising regularly is and always has been the answer and all the other fake substitutes are no more than a temporary solution to a lazy habit. The reality is that the secrets of success are actually the formula for losing weight and staying in shape.

For example, if one truly desires to lose weight and believes it is possible (and believes in themselves), they will commit and do whatever action and effort necessary to accomplish their goal. Will it be hard? Of course.

But the committed individual doesn't set a goal and stick to it for a week, they stick to it forever. Will fear, doubts, criticisms, and possible failures occur? Always.

But the individual who persists and does not quit in their daily healthy eating habits and exercising routine - whether it takes two months or two years - they will succeed.

2) Career Growth: Advancement within a job, company, or career is based much more upon the secrets of success than it is the traditional route our culture commonly and mistakenly believes.

For example, how often have you personally been guilty of thinking that your potential and advancement is determined by networking or connections, the perfect opportunity at the right time, a better prepared resume, unethical practices in order to get recognized, becoming 'buds' with the boss, advanced degrees or certificates earned, or even years on the job?

Each of these certainly is important and has its place (excluding the unethical practices); however, what people often fail to realize is that these situations are secondary to one's desire, belief, and work ethic.

3) Academic Pursuits: First of all, never fall victim to the fallacy that your GPA, major or emphasis studied, standardized test scores, name of the institution attended, or even the degrees you earned (or did not earn) somehow dictate or determine your potential.

If the accomplishment of any goal is based upon these foundational principles that entail the secrets of success, then certainly developing the ability to read, write, study, memorize, retain, present, test well, and intellectually and academically excel must be based upon the same foundational success principles.

4) Spiritual Development: Do not ignorantly assume that these principles apply only to matters of physical or temporal conditions. In order to develop character, pray effectively, worship meaningfully, endure faithfully, and progress spiritually - we absolutely must apply these same principles. Scripturally, belief is faith, action is works, and persistence is enduring to the end.

5) Entrepreneurial Ventures: Often what holds people back from taking risks is not necessarily fear - it is the excuse that they do not have the time, knowledge, or money to pursue their goal or dream.

Anybody who is truly desirous for and committed to accomplishing their goal will make time, obtain the necessary knowledge, and will realize that acquiring wealth does not always require having money initially.

Successful entrepreneurs are not born with increased talent or brains, they succeed because they are willing to take risks, they learn from and persist after failures, the overcome the voices of fear and doubt in their mind, they take daily action and they never quit.

6) Social Abilities: If these principles apply to anything, then why would they not apply to even the development and improvement of our social abilities?

Thus, the ability to make friends can be developed, the fear of public speaking can be overcome, relationships that have been ruined can be fixed, a lack of self-esteem can be improved, feeling comfortable in social settings can be learned, interacting with and approaching others can be done confidently, and a deficiency in verbal and non-verbal communication skills can be mastered.

7) Quitting Addictions & Habits: Are you addicted to drugs, alcohol, pornography, tobacco, video games, etc? Do you have any bad habits that you are desirous to be rid of, or even trying to break currently?

Don't get me wrong, the various addiction recovery groups, cigarette patches, community programs, and self-help books are extremely helpful; but by themselves, they cannot produce the necessary change unless they are combined with an individual's strong desire, belief that it is possible, faith in oneself, daily action, overcoming doubts, and persisting and never quitting until the goal has been accomplished.

8) Financial Management & Wealth Accumulation: Decide now to forever rid yourself of excuses. Your poor financial situation is not the result of family upbringing, lack of education, high interest rates, dishonest brokers or companies, or inability to access funds.

Most likely it is the result of terrible budgeting, an inability to save, a lack of discipline to go without, poor judgment in determining needs vs. wants, and a lack of effort to change your situation.

In addition, your financial future is not determined by an accountant, 401(k) account, the stock market, rich uncle, wise broker, or success on the job. You determine and create your potential - and wealth.

The ability to develop financial discipline is more important than budgets or accounting software. Your potential to become wealthy is based upon desire, belief, and work ethic - not an industry, company, or position.

Your own drive and initiative is of far greater value than the advice given by a greedy broker. Your financial situation and future is created and determined by you, and is enhanced by applying the very secrets of success.

9) Overcoming Challenges: Hospitals are filled, pharmacies are stocked, bookstores are loaded, clinics are full, stores are overflowing, and websites are abundant with information and products that supposedly have the solution to every problem we encounter in life.

Whether it is dealing with depression, sickness or injury, disability, lack of self-esteem, marriage or relationship problems, loneliness, minority set-backs, financial hardships, or even stress - the solution always seems to be in some new product, pill, book, program, doctor's advice, or latest research.

Don't get me wrong, each of these institutions and sources provide tremendous value and certainly have their place; but they fail to educate and provide their consumers with the necessary knowledge, attributes, and actions required to overcome any of the aforementioned challenges we all face.

The ability to control one's thoughts is just as important as the pill used to cure depression. The ability to think big is far more liberating and empowering to one with a disability than any wheelchair or crutch.

Dealing with stress or a lack of self-esteem requires belief and consistent action much more than popping a pill. And the list could go on and on. Is it not obvious that the secrets of success apply even to the ability to deal with and overcome the challenges of life?

The reality is that the secrets of success apply to any situation and pursuit in life - whether it is breaking the chains of poverty, to becoming a professional athlete, to developing a talent, to learning how to sing or play an instrument, to dealing with death or difficulties, these foundational elements that form the secrets of success are the necessary attributes and actions required to accomplish any of our goals, pursuits, challenges, and dreams in life. And they apply to everyone, to every situation, and to every goal.

CHAPTER 43

USE MEDITATION TO MASTER THE ART OF SUCCESS

If you want to be successful, you must train your mind to be successful. You must have an overwhelming belief or faith in yourself that you can do it, even when everyone around you is telling you that you cannot do it. The key to this success is to program you for success.

When I was doing a business course a few months ago one of the tasks that we were given was to write down ten things that we wanted to achieve. We were asked to identify specifically what those ten things are in business we wanted to achieve. The sort of items people wrote down -

1. I am going to make $200,000 cash profit this year

2. I am going to buy a new Mercedes

3. I am going to buy a jet ski

4. I am going to raise $500,000 to build an orphanage in Laos

5. I am going to buy the block Lot 4 Coral Coast Road in Townsville Australia

6. I am going to take my family to Las Vegas and have $5,000 spending money

7. I am going to raise the $4,000 to buy a Vintage Plane for the RAAF Museum

8. I am going to win the Archery at the next Commonwealth Games

9. I am going to learn to fly a plane

10. I am going to hike up Mount Kosciusko

What people were then told was to right these elements down onto a sheet of paper and put them up where you could see them every day where you can read them and remind yourself of what you are going to achieve. Essentially what they told us to do is to follow the third secret to success identified by Napoleon Hill called Autosuggestion.

However, what I noticed with all the people in course was that over a period of time, they began to give up. They did not read their ten items every day and they did not affirm that they would achieve what they wanted each day.

Part of the reason this occurs is simply because the hustle, bustle and stress of everyday life and reality take over and your mind is cluttered with the stress. When the course finished they did not have the people in the course to continually speak with them to see if they were sticking to their ten things they wanted to achieve.

Look ask any educator in the world, if you are stressed when trying to learn something, you will never learn the material as well as somebody who is not stressed.

Why ... because a mind that is not stressed and cluttered will allow you to absorb the information more effectively than somebody who does not and this leads me to how Meditation is one of the secret tools to success.

Meditation on its own will not bring you success. The role of meditation in the art of success is to bring your mind to a point of calm where it can absorb all the material to help you succeed and in particular, so that you can ingrain into your mind the affirmations of what you are going to achieve.

The first step in using meditation to help you succeed is to learn to meditate to eliminate the stress. Before trying to address anything else you must learn to relax and be calm and to clear your mind. That is, your mind must be free from clutter, worry, concerns and anything else that may stop you from programming your mind to succeed.

There are many meditations that will help you in overcoming stress such as the breathing meditation technique, stillness meditation technique and the numbers meditation technique. Each of these techniques will teach you how to achieve focus and calm during your meditation session.

Once you have mastered those techniques, you can then focus on your affirmations or autosuggestions each day of what you are going to achieve.

The Buddhists use sacred phrases in their meditations to help them become better people on their journey towards achieving enlightenment. You can use the affirmations or ten things you want to achieve in exactly the same way.

By reflecting on the ten things you want to achieve during meditation, you are reinforcing what you want to achieve in the way of success and ingraining in a clear mind these affirmations or autosuggestions, which means you will maintain your focus to achieve these ten things even when you are challenged by what is going on in your day.

When you start using this technique over a period of time, you will be amazed how your mind will say to you, "Hey, you are off focus on what you want to achieve get back on focus".

I recommend that for meditation to work effectively that you spend no less than 20 minutes in the morning and night meditating on the 10 things you must achieve.

The reason that I recommend meditating twice a day is that you need to be reflecting on your affirmations for a minimum of 20 minutes a day, however most people find that it takes them about ten minutes of their meditation time before they are truly calm, when they are first starting out.

You will find though as time goes on and you meditate regularly that you are able to get to a state of calm a lot quicker than when you first start out.

Look the bottom line is this, if you want to succeed, you must believe inside of yourself that you can achieve whatever success you want. It is totally up to you as to what you want to achieve and only you can do it.

Remember, that every great achievement in the world started out as a single thought that one person believed in enough to what to achieve it. To stay on the path to success, meditation will help you to control the clutter and the stress the world can pile on you on a day-to-day basis in your mind.

CHAPTER 44

IMITATE THE SECRETS OF SUCCESSFUL PEOPLE

The secret of living a successful in life is what much of the world wants to learn, covet those who attain it, and pursue it. The secrets of successful people prove to us that reaching our objectives brings us incomparable fulfillment and happiness.

A successful and happy life is uncovered by realizing your true free will. That gives us a distinct chance to be happy every day, if we attain small objectives every day and action step by action-taking-step we will be approaching our GREAT dream.

Recollect to your college or high school studies, when you had to combine work and study; when you had an extremely tense schedule. When your only service was a custom-made term paper to get through the semester, I mean.

You stood by it. By attaining mini objectives every term, at last you reached the primary goal-- successful graduation. This is why you are adopting the habits of highly effective individuals by reading this book.

One of the qualities of the secret of being successful in life is always aiming for excellence and never resting on laurels.

Let's go even deeper yet and establish ourselves...

Close your eyes for a minute and imagine an effective individual who understands the secret of being successful in life.

Is he filled with lacking thoughts or abundant?

Surely, most of us associate the law of success with abundant people.

Success and wealth are inseparable from each other? Yes, it's most likely to be so.

Abundant thinking is not a target for a highly effective individual, rather it is just among the steps to reach universal alignment.

Exactly do you believe there are any unbiased factors hindering finding the secret of being successful in life?

We develop the biggest challenge in accomplishing success with our fears, complexes and more negativity based on self-doubt. And then, there is answering to, what is the secret of success?

Let's look at the secrets of successful people:

Clear objectives and goals

Without the aim, no achievement is possible. A thoroughly equipped ship with fantastic crew will get no place if it hasn't any course of direction.

Accurate method of planning

Unplanned success is an organized defeat. Rational and accurate technique helps to recognize the grandest tasks. A successful individual fulfills a small part of his fantastic strategy every day. You will have the ability to manifest whatever you desire if you stay with your strategy. And if you desire, you have a potential.

Positive attitude and optimistic outlook

Positive right-minded thinking and a favorable mindset to the world works wonders. You reside in the world you develop on your own. You want to live in a fantastic world-- think about something wonderful. Stop fretting and hesitating of failures and you will reach your success.

Faith in the secret of being successful in life

Leave all your wrong-minded ego-based fear and self-doubts behind if you have some desire. We all have an ego as humans while in this world, which at times can be compared to a fearful bratty child.

This darkened thought system is constantly hounding us with judgment and criticism, so have your ego thought system take a back seat as your spirit does the driving.

Education and training

Being knowledgeable about your desires with no action taking steps will lead to absolutely nothing. Only actions, supported by knowledge will result in fantastic success. Continuous training, consistent enhancement of your expert understanding, - these are the functions that distinguish a highly effective individual.

Our world is ever transforming and moving for the better, and just on condition of applying your new understanding you will begin aligning to a better life.

Self-- enhancement and personal inner growth

It helps us to change for the better and overcome our complexes and fears due to self-doubt. Remember, that everything depends only on you; you are master of your fate, your success and joy.

And if you don't have all the listed above qualities for the secret of being successful in life, then you will have the ability to develop these features and on to improving yourself.

The only thing that does not depend on you is the Light of your true free will, because you were given it in the Creation. You own it. You will need to simply uncover it because the ego's dark thought system has been obscuring it and your passion most likely has been dim.

Self-- Confidence helps us to get leading results

By letting go of your ego-based complexes, the law of success begins working for you and you begin approaching perfect alignment with the universe to live the life you want.

Now let the Law of Success take over:

This chapter on how successful people grow is merely a discussion on the philosophy of success. These are just words from thoughts, though wise and real about the secret of being successful in life. You are able to turn this approach into an effective tool for enhancing your inner self and moving forward in life.

The law of success will grant you the secrets of successful people where you will benefit from it greatly. This simple viewpoint will become your strategy, your inner thread for achieving success.

CHAPTER 45

SMART GOAL SETTING TO ACHIEVE SUCCESS

In order to effectively achieve your goals in a timely manner, individuals must undergo strategic planning and personal goal setting in order to establish clear agendas.

While there are many different ways to approach such a life-changing path towards success, there is a helpful technique to consider that provides an easy-to-follow tool of motivation known as setting SMART goals.

The concept of SMART goals is based upon specific steps used to encourage one to reach their potential beyond what they believe is attainable.

One of the most important aspects of SMART goals is to set a deadline, which helps keep individuals moving towards accomplishing their business dreams and expectations. Without a deadline, goals face the threat of staying stagnant, but when setting a targeted date for success, motivation becomes stronger.

When you are interested in using SMART goals to achieve success, you should become familiar with the different components that make up this helpful goal-setting plan. Establishing SMART goals means that one approaches their objective in life or business in a (S)pecific, (M)easurable, (A)ttainable, (R)ealistic, and (T)angible manner.

One of the significant aspects of goal setting includes establishing specific goals, which may involve daily, weekly, monthly, or yearly targets. It is a proven fact that those who set goals in life achieve much more than those who do not (no matter how frequent they are set).

These goals should be measurable, as this helps one gauge how easy it would be to achieve such desires. When goals are vaguely set, it is hard to measure how long it will take to accomplish such objectives.

Setting attainable goals usually involves the things in life and business that are most important, which encourages you to reach them quicker and more easily. This is because when something is significant to your happiness and success in life, you are much more apt to find a way towards achievement.

Naturally, you will seek out the steps that fit into your goals and with a positive attitude as your driving force - you slowly (or steadily) work on using your knowledge to develop the skills that enable you to succeed.

Some obstacles, such as financial capability, often comes into play, yet motivated individuals have a knack for discovering new and improved ways on accomplishing the things they want out of life.

The key to successfully reaching goals is to plan the steps needed to reach positive results. A set timeframe also serves as a powerful motivating tool and plays a key role in setting SMART goals. Setting realistic goals is also an important part of the SMART goal setting process, as it is quite hard to reach something that is far too out of attainability.

When setting goals, they should remain within the realm of possibility. An example of an unrealistic goal is to plan on climbing the highest peak in the world when you are physically unable to achieve this type of objective. This may include an issue with having seizures when reaching high altitudes.

Despite the advancements in technology (Internet, email, medicine, science), some goals are simply impossible. These types of goals should be avoided, as realistic goals will only reap satisfaction when achieved.

A tangible goal is one that is recognized by at least one of your five senses. This means that if you are able to taste, touch, hear, see, or smell a specific goal, it is something tangible.

For those who are able to incorporate a tangible goal with one that is intangible, they face a better chance of pinpointing the things that makes an objective more specific and measurable. In the end, you will encounter something that is much more attainable in the long run.

In order to get you on the right track for setting SMART goals, consider implementing some of the following tips to make your journey towards success much easier:

1. Being specific with your goal setting is seen through the strong statements you make about your objectives. An example of setting a challenging, yet motivating goal is to exclaim, "I will move to California by the end of the year to pursue acting," instead of "I want to be in a movie."

2. Phrasing your SMART goals in the present tense helps pull you closer towards achieving success. Get out of the habit of saying "I want to" and start saying, "I will." This will help you approach your objectives in a manner that is more susceptible to accomplishment.

3. Writing down your SMART goals is a great way to clarify your objectives and create a better visualization of the outcome. Some individuals will jot down each goal on a separate index card, which they then review on a daily basis. This serves as a motivating reminder.

4. When you list the benefits you expect to receive out of achieving a SMART goal, this helps to keep you steadfast in your intentions; increases focus and makes obstacles much easier to overcome.

For instance, a person listing the benefits for losing weight may review the positive aspects when they feel a weakness to binge on sweets. The more advantages you are able to come up with, the more motivating the goals will become.

CHAPTER 46

GOAL SETTING AND YOUR STRENGTHS

If you set and achieve daily goals, this will add up to some major goal accomplishments at the end of the year. And it's all your own work. Happy people take control of their lives, rather than just drifting or let others make the decisions. Recognize the feeling of control and empowerment as you establish and then accomplish your goals.

Imagine you have a deadline at work (something you cannot control). However, how would it be if you made the decision to meet that deadline ahead of time? Or if you are the sort of person that tends to go over deadlines, making excuses all the way, turn this around and work hard to meet that deadline.

Recognize how much you can do. Even a shift in attitude can give a feeling of mastery. Being able to overcome hurdles and developing a more constructive attitude to the things you cannot control is a great confidence booster.

Flow experience

By setting yourself regular, meaningful goals you position yourself to encounter more flow experiences. A flow experience is one where your whole consciousness is absorbed with a particular activity.

Thoughts of time and other needs (such as hunger) are forgotten. Positive psychologists generally agree that the more flow experiences a person has, the happier they are. Goals give us something we can actively get involved with, which is an essential ingredient to a flow experience.

To achieve this state it is important to have a clear purpose. So clearly defining your goals is a good start. Also, you will want to choose a goal that is challenging for you, but is not out of your depth. If it is not challenging enough, you will almost certainly become bored.

It is worth reviewing your goals on a regular basis to help keep you motivated. Furthermore, try to obtain regular feedback so you are aware of how you are doing. Support from others can be a good idea, else make sure you track your progress in some way.

Goals and the flow experience have a good relationship. By setting goals we enhance our chances of experiencing flow. By experiencing flow, we are more likely to achieve our goals.

General wellbeing

Having goals in our life is good for our wellbeing. It provides us with an opportunity to go on a journey which we can learn from and enjoy. It helps a person appreciate their capabilities, gives life a purpose and increases optimism.

As such, it can reduce stress and help reduce the chances of developing depression. Carrying out goal-related tasks gives a person focus and increases happiness.

Goal setting and your strengths

When setting and working on your goals, consider how you might use your personal strengths to help you achieve your objectives. It is worth knowing what your top strengths are as these are the ones that are most effortless to use and so drawing on them should be a great motivator.

Consider how the following strengths may assist you when setting up your goals:

Curiosity, creativity and love of learning may assist you in your brainstorming. This may be useful when you are considering which goals to set, how you are going to achieve them and ways to overcome potential difficulties.

Bravery can help you reach for those huge goals you've never quite got off the ground. This strength will enable you to act, in spite of your misgivings. If persistence is your strength, then you are sure to achieve the goals you set yourself. Having humor as your strength will enable you to laugh if things go wrong, as you see the lighter side of life.

Prudence can help you set the right goals as you are able to consider whether the goal you think you want now is one you will want in the future. Being authentic means you will remain true to yourself when setting your goals. It ensures you are doing them for yourself and not other people.

Another way you can make use of personal strengths when setting goals, is to actually set a goal dedicated to developing a particular strength. For instance, you might want to work on being kinder, so decide to volunteer at an organization that helps other people.

Alternatively, you could use goal setting as an opportunity to nurture a particular strength, although the strength is not a goal in itself. For instance your goal is to write a novel.

However, along the way you decide to exercise your gratitude strength and so make a conscious effort to acknowledge those people who assisted you in working towards your goal. Whatever goals you set yourself, enjoy the process and think how they are benefiting you along the way.

CHAPTER 47

MAKING A RESOLUTION

We now know that motivation is the key to getting things done; for achieving goals and desires. We also know that aligning our motif with our values is important.

People often say: 'I know it is important to me but I am just not that motivated'. These people rarely start or change anything because they are waiting to be motivated first. They somehow think that the only way they can move towards something (or away from something) is to be motivated. Wrong.

They somehow expect that motivation will appear out of thin air and this will magically hurdle them into action towards their goal. Don't sit around waiting for motivation to magically appear...it doesn't and it won't. The motivation bus will never arrive no matter how long you wait for it.

What follows is a most important statement.

DON'T wait to feel, or to get, motivated

If what you want to achieve is important to you and you don't feel motivated, just do it anyway without feeling motivated. Make the decision to do it. Yes this might take an act of will, discipline and determination. Yes it might be unpleasant, require a commitment and you might even have to give up something else.

Yet you do it because you know the end result, your goal and that is more important than whether you feel motivated or not. The problem is that most people focus on what they have to give up rather than focussing on the long term gain.

Do you really think elite swimmers look forward to getting up every morning at 4:30am day after day? Rather than begrudging their early morning starts, they are completely focused on the end result; their goal. That is what keeps them going, that is what motivates them.

What is important to you?

When you want to achieve something that is important to you, just start the ball rolling. Start pushing that motivation ball until it creates its own momentum...and it will, and then it might even be hard to stop.

As the famous Nike motto says 'Just Do It.' Or as the famous quote attributed to Johann Wolfgang von Goethe says: 'Whatever you can do or dream you can, begin it. Boldness has genius, power and magic in it'.

Just like starting to exercise again after you haven't for a while or perhaps never. It is highly unlikely that you will jump out of bed one morning full of motivation and start exercising.

You might not feel like it, but because you know it is important, you will feel better and healthier in the long term, you get going even though you don't want to. At first it is a real effort and you might have to fight that little voice in your head that will offer you all kinds of good reasons and temptations not to do it.

Here is an important fact. The more you do it, the more motivated you will become. The more the ball gets pushed, the more the ball will create its own momentum. It's just like pushing a rock up hill. When you push a rock up on one side of a hill, it gets harder and harder the closer you get to the top.

Most people give up just before the critical moment of breakthrough. But when you push that rock over the edge it creates its own momentum and it will roll down faster and faster as it builds up more momentum.

So remember. You won't always be motivated to do the things that are important to you. Don't wait for motivation to come along. Make a decision to do it anyway and start creating momentum. Soon you will find that the momentum will continue all on its own and it might even pull you along with it.

CHAPTER 48

IDEAS TO STAY FOCUSED AND ON PURPOSE

When you first bring your profession home and begin your stay at home business, you will soon yearn for that tiny little cubicle that you had when you were at an office working for someone else. At least when you were in your own cubicle, you were able to turn your back on impositions and get your work done.

However, in an at home atmosphere, this does not always happen. When working for an employer, usually it was a nine to five job where your productivity did not have that much influence on your paycheck at the end of the week.

This is not so with your own business. Your salary is directly proportional to your productivity. You will need to learn early on in your business how to combat these interruptions, stay focused and on task or you will not be in business for yourself for very long.

To be able to overcome your distractions, you will need to recognize where they are coming from. Are they self-imposed or are they from family and friends? One self-imposed distraction that can be extremely disruptive is procrastination. It is also easy to fall off task when we have too many interests and try to do all of them at once.

This may seem like multi-tasking but really you are just spinning your wheels and exhausting yourself. Self-inflicted distractions are the most difficult to conquer but it can be done. By following a few simple steps, you will have no problem winning against the time wasters.

1. Quiet Time: It is not necessary to step into your office and become involved in the first task on hand immediately. Take a moment to sit and look at your computer and look out of the window. Better yet, step outside for a moment in the morning sun and clear your mind of the daily family activities.

This is what you would normally do on your commute from your home to a normal job at an office. Take ten minutes in the morning to begin the transition from family/house life to work life. Begin to think about the projects that are a priority for the day.

2. Create a To Do List: After you have spent a moment "commuting" to work, begin to create a to do list of the projects and tasks that need to be done. It is okay to add to this list throughout the day for additional items that you might have forgotten about.

When creating your list, do not just write down a general idea of the project. Give your task a name and break it into milestones. This will eliminate procrastination and make the task easier to manage. This is especially important for long-term projects. Each time you cross off an item on your todo list, it will give you a feeling of accomplishment.

3. Have a Set Schedule for Tasks: Most employees have a set time to work such as your old "nine to five" job. It is also important to follow this same rule when working from home. Have a set time that you will begin work and close up shop at a certain time.

Since you own the business, you can choose if you want to work ten hours straight through or break your day into two work periods of five hours each. Also, set a fixed time to answer your email and other daily tasks.

You do not have to answer every email that comes to you within minutes of receiving it. Sometimes it is even easier to just turn off your email program all together until your set time.

4. Shut the Door. With smaller children, you will need to address each issue as the need arises. That is not so with older children. They will understand when you tell them you need to work from x to y. Hire an in-home babysitter for younger children or enlist an aunt or grandparent if possible.

If the phone becomes a distraction, turn the ringer off for an hour so that you can concentrate on your task. Most of all, do not permit family and friends to distract them. Be firm with them and let them know that you are at work and cannot be disturbed for x amount of time. You will be glad you did.

CHAPTER 49

BUILD CONFIDENCE AND REACH YOUR GOALS THROUGH "FLOW"

Flow has been described as "an investment in ourselves to our limits." We've all experienced the thrill of "flow" at some point in our lives. During those times of "flow" every obstacle seems to disappear, and we are in love with what we are doing so much that it seems effortless. Flow can be experienced in any area of your life.

Much has been written in the dating community about the idea of "getting into state." Hell, I've even wrote a post titled "Seven Secrets to Getting into State".

But I am beginning to see that the true super achievers, top athletes, master pickup artists, and billion dollar executives have been able to maintain this state over longer periods of time. Because the "state" doesn't come and go at will, it turns into a sort of flow...

Getting to flow in your life means achieving a state of concentration so total that everything else becomes non- existent. It is about becoming so engrossed in your activities that they transform into a sort of meditation. It is the experience of knowing that you're 100% in the current moment, not only in body, but also in mind and spirit.

The many great thinkers who have studies flow have found there to be five general secrets to getting into the state of flow regularly.

1. Have a purpose in life that you are passionate about.

Once you become clear about where you are headed in life... and a strong desire to get there, you will notice that you'll transform into the activity you are currently doing.

For instance, as I am writing this to you, I've slowly become the act of writing. I am no longer a body with a mind trying to figure out what to write... I've actually become these words appearing on the computer screen talking to you.

2. Clear Your Mind of all distractions and focus entirely on the present.

It is so tempting to take yourself out of the current moment with thoughts of what happened yesterday, what you have to do tomorrow, or what you'd rather be doing right now. Even as you're reading this you might only be partially digesting it, ready to skim through and move on to the next email.

But, understand, you have more time than you think. And once you get fully involved with what you're doing, you'll find that time literally stands still. This is how come the super high achievers are able to reach such high levels. They've learned to manipulate time by eliminating distractions.

3. Let go

Resist your desire to strive for what you want. I've continually found, especially with women that the minute I stop striving for what I consciously believe I want. What I truly want finds me.

This requires surrendering to the process. Fall in love with act of meeting new people, develop a genuine curiosity about human nature and suddenly results won't mean nearly as much.

Once you stop worrying about winning and losing, you'll find that your mind finds the peace it needs. And with the "peace" comes a rooted, unshakeable, and unbreakable confidence that raises you to levels you never knew existed.

4. Enjoy the process

A few years ago I began taking salsa lessons. The first couple lessons I was completely frustrated by my lack of progress. I was thinking too much about "how long it would take to get good." I was comparing myself to some of the other dancers in the class and wondering what I was missing.

It wasn't until my fourth class that I finally was able to let go. Once I let go, I put my entire mind into the process of learning each new step. And as I fully focused solely on learning the next step... I began to really enjoy the process.

5. Don't fight the bliss

As you sense that you're reaching that peak productivity without striving... simply let it happen. Don't question it. Don't stop to take notes of how you got there. In fact, as you begin to realize you are in flow, simply acknowledge the thought, and dive right back into the process.

I would be lying if I said that I was at the point where I could reach "flow" at will. But I know that following those steps have gotten me there much more often.

I never get anywhere, and it always feels like a struggle to stay motivated to write. But once I simply focus on each word, and concentrate one sentence at a time on communicating to my intended reader as clearly and as passionately as possible, I begin to get lost in the moment.

No matter what you're looking to achieve, dating more women, finding a girlfriend, making more money, losing weight, you'll find that by following the five steps above not only will the process be more enjoyable, but by staying focused in the moment, you will be taking the steps you need to reach your goal.

CHAPTER 50

STAY FOCUSED AND MOTIVATED WHEN IT REALLY COUNTS

Staying in focus is one of the most difficult skills to acquire, no matter whether you are taking an examination, training for a sports race or building a business. If you can laser focus on one specific subject and learn it inside and out, you will achieve unbelievable levels in whatever you chose to get involved in.

I should explain the term, "When it matters most." as this is very important and can relate to many different things. If you set aside one hour to write a note, then you should rarely allow anything to disturb that hour. You will end up wasting your time and become unproductive.

But you shouldn't aim your focus totally at one thing for long periods of time, as this will inevitably end in frustration. If your goal is to complete one hour of study, then one hour it is and no more.

You will then need to take a break and not overdo it, because if you continue to spend too much time on one thing, you will reduce your capacity to get the job completed smoothly.

What are the particular obstacles that will destroy your focus?

There are many challenges, problems and obstacles that will ace your future and take your focus away from your goal or target. Allowing things like the telephone, neighbors, friends, family, social networking or emails to control your time and knock you off of your perch.

You must ensure that you control your environment and the people around you, so that you refuse to allow any form of distraction to upset the fine and delicate balance when you are in flow. Here are the 5 keys to staying focused and motivated.

Eliminate the static in your life

This means having the ability to identify all of the distractions that will destroy your focus and then eliminating them as rapidly as you can and permanently. But realize that some distractions may have to be worked on over time. This is crucial if you are to get to the very top at anything or become one of the best at what you do.

Learn the art of concentration

This relates to the art of concentrating one single solitary project, similar to an archer or an Olympic high jumper or bird watcher. You must zero in your focus on the target at hand and not allow anyone or anything to block your vision or disturb the balance of your concentration.

Add passion to your emotional desires

The reasons that you begin a task or start training for the marathon or similar, are critical. They must be emotional reasons that get you excited and passionate about the journey and the pending outcome. To be effective these reasons have to be extremely strong, bordering on obsession.

Create a habit of allowing your powerful focus to motivate you.

Your motivation to stay on target and focus will come from inside. Do let anyone else have the job of motivating you, because you will always be the best motivator that you will find. If you are not motivated enough to learn the skill or habit of focus, then examine the reasons why you are doing what you are doing.

Teach yourself to stay on target regardless

This very simply means keeping your focus, come what may and feeling good about it. Most people have to teach themselves how to use focus and then they have to learn to keep their eyes on that one project only. This is a learned skill that may take some considerable time to master.

It is your responsibility not to lose focus at any time and remember to rest if you need to recharge your batteries before continuing. Even the best soldiers can only focus for short periods of time. Also consider using the power of the mastermind or mentoring if you require any assistance in the area of focus and motivation.

CHAPTER 51

TIME MASTERY TIPS

Time mastery is different from time management. Time management is simply managing the time you have to work with each day and sometimes involves getting more done in less time.

Time mastery on the other hand has first and foremost to do with being proactive and deciding in advance what you want (goals), how you will set up your days (your life really), and then choosing the best ways to execute that.

Below are time mastery tips that may help you on your new journey. All of them are proven to help you visualize what you really want, focus on what's most important to you now, say "no" to the things that get in the way of that, help free up time, create more efficiency, bring a sense of order and peace to a daily routine, and offer a sense of control. They work.

This is a list, not a plan. The list includes 40 strategies that will allow you to create the life you want in terms of how you use your time. They may or may not all be fitting for your life.

Simply choose the ones that make sense to you-perhaps all of them will. Factor them into your routine, and implement them without hesitation. They will make your life and business more meaningful, easier and more enjoyable.

1. Establish a list of your important long-term, mid-term, and short-term goals. Select the MOST important one from each category-the one that you want to focus on AT THIS TIME IN YOUR LIFE. You will have 3 to focus on at a time (one from each category).

2. Write your goals down: Written goals help the subconscious mind to work towards goal accomplishment and greatly increase the likelihood of achieving them. Written goals can be changed or adjusted at any time.

3. Create a list of tasks or activities that would cause you to accomplish each goal.

4. Prioritize your tasks and activities. The 80-20 Rule of economist Vilfredo Pareto notes that 80 percent of the reward comes from 20 percent of the effort. Prioritize tasks in order of value and importance. Concentrate on those items with the greatest reward-getting you to your goal.

5. Assign a deadline to projects and tasks, particularly the ones that will take multiple activities to complete. Don't fret-deadlines can be changed. Just do your best.

6. Think about tasks as being made up of "Time Molecules". Some are small and some are bigger molecules. These "molecules" are "chunks" of time you can spend on a task throughout a day or on different days. Work on projects and tasks in "time molecule" chunks to finish at the deadline.

7. Revisit and declare your long-term and mid-term goals periodically, such as once a year on New Years day or your birthday: your desires may change, so your goals may dramatically change at any point in your life. For short-term goals, you should have a planning session at least every 3 months.

8. Two or more goals can be of the same importance even though you spend different amounts of time on each. You may have to set one goal temporarily aside while you work towards another, but acknowledge that they are both still goals and both still important.

9. Use only one calendar and look at it often. Use a day planner. Choose a simple one. Complicated systems can cause you to waste time while planning. Keep your planner with you at all times.

10. Before scheduling activities, block out family and personal time first. Block out time for vacation, spa days, exercise, personal time, church, and family. Block out events and trade shows that involve your career. Find the info from magazines and online.

11. Review your goals daily. Spend evenings (or early mornings) planning and organizing your approaching day. 15 minutes is enough time. Try to find solitude. Select and schedule some of the activities that will help to propel you towards your most important priority goals. these activities will be your high priority tasks.

12. Have a running to-do list, a single page or two in your day planner to jot down tasks that you suddenly remember have to be done. Try to schedule a few of these tasks into your daily activities. Delegate as many as possible.

13. Use a daily to-do list for what you want to accomplish each day. This will be the list you make during your daily planning session. Each day, schedule some of the priority tasks needed to achieve your goals and some from your "Running-To-Do-List". Keep your daily tasks reasonable in number and achievable. Keep in mind you will experience interruptions.

14. Prioritize your daily to-do list items in terms of value and importance; #1 is the most important and valuable to accomplish, #2 the second most, etc. Keep your goals in mind. If you can't do a task in order of priority because of time or other constraints, move to the next number and come back to the highest priority task later. Again, delegate where you can.

15. Commit to do the items on your list, cross out tasks that have been accomplished.

16. Start the day with a high-priority task and continue with it until it is complete whenever you can. Focus on your most valuable task or activity in relation to your goals. You feel happier, more productive, and more in control of your life.

17. Block out a chunk of uninterrupted time in the same time slot each day to work on high priority tasks. Focus your attention and work on several similar or related tasks during this time (called batching). 1-3 hours is ideal.

18. Remember the concept of MOMENTUM if you are tempted to procrastinate. Just say you will work on a task for 2 minutes with no guilt if you stop. You will likely continue.

19. Schedule your most important tasks during your naturally productive time of the day. Do not use up your "Best Time" to do low priority or mundane tasks that can be done any time of day (or by someone else).

20. Schedule in at least a few small tasks that you will complete in a day. This will empower and motivate you as you check them off your list.

21. Delegate tasks that are low priority or those others can easily do. Spend money to save time. Tasks that require little specialized training can be delegated out to office assistants. Tasks that require expertise can be sent out to a professional company.

You can also hire out for personal chores such as dog walking, or things you do not like to do such as laundry. This will free you up. Look at it as a financial investment-Comparative Advantage- spend YOUR time on the things that make you the most profit and delegate the rest. Make the most money with your time.

22. Invest time in training others. Give up time in the short-term to train others for long-term benefits.

23. DO NOT let email overtake you. Check your mail once a day, or if you must once in the morning and once in the evening only. Set up a direct reply auto-responder letting people know you will get back to them within "blank number" of hours.

24. Totally eliminate time wasters like tasks that don't propel you towards your goals, don't relax you, and don't make you feel good about your life.

25. Refuse to be caught in the trap of perfectionism. Perfectionism gets in the way of productivity. It means you are paying unnecessary attention to detail. You likely are the only one who knows the difference. This form of procrastination can keep you from accomplishing your true goals.

26. Leave a little bit of "free" time in your day for unexpected interruptions and time intrusions, and for opportunities that may come up. This is real life, be flexible when scheduling (but also be responsible).

27. Minimize interruptions by isolating yourself. Find a place to "hide away" for a few hours.

28. Focus on one task or activity at a time. Have out ONLY what you are CURRENTLY working on.

29. Avoid big lunches that can make you sluggish for the rest of the day.

30. Schedule time with your customers for when it is most convenient for THEM (it can really improve your sales results).

CHAPTER 52

OUR ENEMY WITHIN

We're all semi-well aware of what self-sabotage is, you know that "spanner" that we throw in our own works, the one that usually finds itself getting firmly lodged between where we are in life and the things that we want the most?

Whether it's a career that completely fulfills us, a healthy and well-balanced relationship, or even a house on a hill with a whopping big Land rover Discovery parked in the driveway, none of us could put hand on heart and state that we are 100% completely content in absolutely every area of our lives.

So why is it that certain things in life seem to be constantly out of our reach for us? Perhaps we find ourselves reaching a particular goal or temporary objective, only to have it mysteriously taken from our grasp for 9 times out of ten, reasons completely unknown to us.

To understand this we must first understand our often highly destructive self-sabotaging nature.

Imagine this, there's something that you want so badly that you'd do anything in order to obtain it, your mind will unconsciously set the wheels of thought in motion to devise the best structured plan in order to make it happen.

Once the plan's in place, the mind activates and determines how you feel about this goal, which becomes the driving forces behind every action you take towards reaching your ultimate goal.

So, your body begins carrying out the mind's instructions. Your mind and body are in sync, an at this stage you've completely mobilized yourself, the machinery is humming along smoothly and you feel on top of the world until something unthought-of happens:

something deep down inside catches wind of your strategic operation and suddenly realizes this new activity stands to potentially threaten your comfort zone.

At this point your primary objective becomes safety. The safety zone is the comfort zone and when you're operating outside of these parameters, the mind becomes completely plagued by doubts, fears or failure, insecurity and low confidence (or as medical professionals might suggest; psychological homeostasis).

When the human mind believes that it's comfort zone is being threatened it "acts out" in all sorts of various ways to restore equilibrium and keeping inner peace (I.e. dropping the ball just before completing an important project, instigating a major fight just when it's clear the relationship could last, drinking the night before the exam, going on a spending spree the first time you have extra money available to put towards your financial future). Sound familiar?

But why is it that so many of us can find ourselves guilty (even on a daily basis) of completely sabotaging our very best intensions? Would the unconscious mind see this exciting new challenge, opportunity or new activity that promises a richer and fuller way of living life as a threat?

Absolutely, and herein lies the key.

When we step out and attempt something new for the first time, we experience an inner conflict between the new picture of how you could see yourself being, and how we're used to being in the past. When tension is successfully managed, it will actually aid in propelling you toward whatever the goal is that you're pursuing.

Without this awareness, it's inevitable that our 'inner person' will "act out" to relieve the tension we're experiencing in order to restore equilibrium (and get back into the comfort zone). So how do we successfully manage the tension?

Consider how self-sabotaging can damage our relationships? It takes two to tango and in order for a relationship to progress healthily, it requires both members to be committed towards investing 100% of who they are truly are into the relationship.

But this doesn't always happen, and if you're anything like me, you probably haven't experienced this kind of relationship throughout your life, because we're all innately and naturally selfish.

When I say that we're all selfish; what we're all fundamentally driven by is having our own innermost needs met. When we're looking for a potential partner to enter into a relationship with or we've chosen someone, we're going to have a series of expectations. We expect to feel secure when we feel significant and when we feel valued by this person.

Recently a guy came on the phone to me who was facing trauma and crisis in his life because he'd found out his long-term partner had been cheating on him.

As you can imagine, he was absolutely broken, he felt completely insignificant and that his partner valued this other man far more than she had ever valued him. He had expected that they would get married and stay together forever, but he hadn't got what he expected, so the trauma wasn't wrapped up in what he found but in his expectations not being met.

I asked him what it was that initially attracted him to his now ex-partner, and he told me he'd met her in a bar and she'd just stood out and he knew she was the one. As we know by now, attraction is not a particularly strong foundation on which to build a relationship, because we're looking for people who are genuine.

Entering into a relationship with someone based upon their looks and how they conduct themselves is all quite superficial and yes, this is important because there has to be an element of physical attraction, but this man was looking for a life partner who would complement him and this didn't work out, because she found a more attractive trophy.

His self-esteem and self-worth was crushed and he didn't feel like a full man anymore because this woman he thought he loved had rejected him for shallow and superficial reasons, possibly the same reasons he had entered into the relationship with her in the first place.

There are two perspectives we can take when entering into a relationship and one is of selfishness, and most of us are naturally selfish. Is this person going to make us feel significant and of value? Will we feel secure with this other person?

When I said that this man was experiencing crisis, we could more accurately describe it as complete mental and emotional collapse. When I asked him how he could sum up the feeling he said that it felt like hell. This happens because sometimes we look to other people to prop us up and be the ones that can hold us up and be our rock in the midst of hard times.

The problem with this is that we're looking to someone or something else on the outside of us to sustain and hold up what's on the inside of us, because our needs aren't on the outside, they're all on the inside.

If this person we look to isn't prepared to take responsibility or ownership of our expectations (which they have no obligation to do), this will, can and does leave us in the midst of crisis that can sometimes be defined as hell on earth. I've been there and there's a good chance you've experienced your version as well.

The guy I've mentioned lived in Manchester (which has a reputation for being quite high in crime) so I asked him if he would go into a bar in one of the less desirable areas of town and leave his wallet on the bar as he went to the toilet, and then in turn expect it to still be there on his return?

He agreed that he wouldn't expect it to be there, so I asked him if he would go to a restaurant that had failed environmental inspections and expect to be served a freshly made healthy meal and not leave with food poisoning.

He said that he wouldn't go there in the first place. You wouldn't expect a dirty restaurant to serve you healthy food and you wouldn't expect it to take responsibility for your expectations, in the same way that you wouldn't expect thieves to take responsibility for your financial wellbeing and not take the money from your wallet.

Why then would we expect another innately selfish human being to make our expectations their responsibility?

There is absolutely nothing on earth that we can control. We can't control how other people act or behave towards us and all we can really take responsibility for in life is our own expectations. It's naïve and irresponsible for us to expect other people to take responsibility for us and vice versa.

My expectations are mine, and yours are yours and they will not always be met. It's when they aren't met that we will experience crisis, trauma and stress in the context of our relationships, so to minimize this and reduce this, we've got to be aware of the kind of people we're entering into relationships with initially, and why we're doing this.

If we're fundamentally entering into a relationship for potentially who they can be for us and what needs of us they can meet, then it's all about us. In the face of crisis, you're not disappointed based upon what you found out, it's all about your expectations not being met.

The only thing that we have any control over in life what so ever is how we choose to respond and react to the situations, circumstances and the relationships that we find ourselves in.

Relationships are developed over time and founded upon trust, so again, why would we ever enter into a committed intimate relationship with someone we don't even know we can trust?

Choosing our relationships wisely is key, and if they're worthy of our trust and friendship, we'll then be able to healthily base our expectations upon results we can see.

This involves both parties to be giving 100% and a very healthy perspective to build your relationships upon is not one of expectations of the other person, but one of responsibility, where the only thing that you can take responsibility for is simply being yourself.

If you don't want to be in a relationship with a cheat or a liar, with someone who's controlling and dishonest, you've got to raise our standards in terms of what you're willing to take responsibility for. We need to be able to take responsibility for ourselves until the right time when we find that right, healthy, meaningful relationship.

Remember the unconscious mind is similar to a computer; it already has firm pictures and beliefs about you and the world. Through careful and through self-exploration we can excavate and examine the contents of our unconscious, discarding the erroneous beliefs that are culturally programmed, handed down by our parents, and formulated by our childhood environment and limited and distorted childhood perception.

It is in doing this that we begin to know freedom, in our work, our relationships, our thinking, and throughout the rest of our lives.

CHAPTER 53

ELIMINATE NEGATIVE AND FEEL GOOD

It seems too simple, I know. It's so simple that we want to make it more difficult, more esoteric. However, the simple truth is that the only way to feel good is to think thoughts that feel good. Likewise, the only way to feel bad is to think thoughts that feel bad. It really is that straightforward.

Because our thoughts produce our feelings, what we choose to think determines how we feel. Please notice it's what we choose to think. Sometimes it doesn't feel like we're choosing our thoughts because negative momentum appears to be choosing our thoughts for us.

Negative momentum may at times feel like a runaway train. We may even be tempted to believe those negative thoughts. However, at any moment, we can consciously choose to think a thought that feels better. Even if we choose a thought that feels just a little bit better, we have stopped the negative momentum and we're re-focused in a more positive direction.

We often want to blame other people or external circumstances for our bad mood. We think, "if only he / she / it would change, I would feel good." Alas, it's up to us. And that is where our power lies. We are guaranteed to feel bad if we think thoughts that feel bad. Likewise, we're guaranteed to feel good if we think good feeling thoughts.

Feeling good really is as easy as thinking thoughts that feel good [or a little bit better], focusing on things that are easy to appreciate and thinking of others who are easy to love. In this way, we begin climbing back up the emotional scale.

It is simple and it does work, but it also takes practice. As we practice choosing thoughts that feel good and we get in the habit of feeling good, pretty soon feeling bad will be so unacceptable that, at the first hint of negative emotion, we'll nip it in the bud and get back to our natural state of well-being.

We all want to feel good and, thankfully, the Law of Attraction teaches us how to do that. We know how to feel good and we have the power to feel good. What could be better than that.

It is. But not the choice you probably think it is. "Stuff happens, moods and feelings happen, emotions happen, it's how it is. Sometimes I feel good and sometimes not...right?"

Feelings don't just happen, you create them.

You feel good when certain things happen and bad when other things happen. You feel good when you're wearing a new shirt. You go out and you're walking on golden wisps of happy sunshine, owning the night. Then your lucky shirt breaks. Why?

The shirt was never lucky. You made it lucky. Really. You decided that it was your lucky shirt. Then it wears off, pardon the pun, when you've worn it a few times or whatever other condition that you've made up for it to not make you feel good anymore is fulfilled.

What made you feel good was the meaning you attached to the shirt. Same thing with everything.

Everything that happens is neutral. Like Switzerland or the color beige. Neutral. Everything that happens is as it is. Even the most heart-wrenching or magnificently glorious moment is just a situation. You feel things about it because you make it into a story and you're invariably the star of the story so it seems super important but it's still just a story. Just a situation.

You feel good or bad because you attach meaning to that situation. What's interesting is that it's all automated, this whole system of giving meaning to situations and feeling a certain way as a result. It's so automated that we don't even notice it happening.

See, you have a certain set of rules or conditions in your mind that when certain things happen, you feel good. And other things that happen make you feel bad.

But then if feeling good is something you're creating when certain things happen, why not just drop the whole condition thing and feel good all the time? Throw a spanner in the automated process of giving meaning to things and stop letting how you feel be controlled by it.

Might be tough at first to allow yourself to feel good all the time but what you can do is to stay neutral and not attach meaning to whatever happens. When something bad happens, it happens. It doesn't mean anything unless you make it mean something.

Stop creating stories about things that happen. Stop giving things meaning. Things happen. It's done. Let it go. When something seemingly bad happens, it's just a situation. Don't call it good or bad. See it for what it is a situation. Creating stories, creating feelings about it will make you feel worse. Just stay neutral about it.

Whenever something happens and you feel an emotion come over you, literally imagine and feel yourself becoming transparent, almost as though you dissolve so that the feeling can't get trapped in you. You don't grab whatever happens and turn it into a feeling, it just gently goes through you and dissolves.

You don't even need to choose to give things positive meanings to make yourself feel good ala "seeing the best in everything" because feeling good isn't about creating the feeling. It's about not creating other feelings that cover up your natural state of limitless bliss. Feeling good is your natural state.

When you stop making things important and allowing your feelings to be controlled by what happens, you stop covering the indescribable magnificence of your true nature - essence of feeling good, the source of all good feeling and you are reconnect to that which you are, instead of thinking that you are your stories. You stop making yourself feel bad and you feel good all the time.

It's not about trying to feel good all the time. It's not about trying to feel anything. The idea is to stop giving meaning to situations so that you can experience the situation instead of the stories and feelings you create about it. Contrary to the title, it's not even about making a choice to feel good.

The choice is to stop layering things over true experience, and that feels good. A whole lot better than manufactured good feeling.

CHAPTER 54

LET YOUR EMOTIONS BE YOUR GUIDE

There really is nothing more important than feeling good. If you think that's a bit of a sweeping statement, just tell me what you think is more important. I'll bet that anything you manage to name would be important for the very fact that it makes you feel good.

Good relationships, making a contribution, serving others, satisfying work, enjoyable pastimes, saving the world - all important because they make us feel good.

Feeling good is an indication that we are aligned with the universal flow of energy. If we can go with the flow and allow our abundance we will effortlessly attract more good things to us. Like attracts like and this is the fundamental principle of the law of attraction.

What we experience in life is a reflection of what we are thinking about most of the time, be it good or bad. "All that we achieve and all that we fail to achieve is the direct result of our own thoughts."

The law of attraction doesn't differentiate between thoughts of what we want and what we don't want. Worrying about an anticipated calamity is the same to our mind as actually experiencing that situation (not just once, but again and again as our mind dwells on it) and as the thoughts multiply so we come closer and closer to actually manifesting the disaster.

As we worry, we feel worse and move ourselves even further from alignment with what we actually want and our connection with the Source.

Don't panic - there is a fool-proof way of getting ourselves back on track. We need to learn to listen to our emotions. Our emotions are indicators of how closely we are aligned with our non-physical higher selves or Source energy and where we are positioned in the natural downstream flow of abundance and well-being.

We have to put our canoe into the stream and let go of the oars. Our emotions will let us know if we need to change our thought pattern.

There's an emotional scale which ranges all the way from despair, grief and fear, through revenge, anger, frustration, and pessimism, into hopefulness, optimism, believing and finally love. It doesn't matter at which point on the scale we enter the stream, we will feel a sense of relief when we start to flow downstream.

We need to remember as well that if we're in the depths of despair we can't expect to be able to jump suddenly up to a state of hopefulness or optimism. We need to move along the scale by finding a slightly better thought to concentrate on which allows us to feel better.

Fear to anger is a common example - if we're frightened, once the shock or danger has passed, the fear easily turns to anger as this does actually make us feel better.

If we feel bad it's because our emotions are telling us that what we are thinking is not aligned to our desires and it's a warning that we must change our thoughts. When we experience pure love we are totally in the flow and experiencing life as it should be enjoyed. This is our ultimate destination.

CHAPTER 55

LIFT YOUR SPIRITS TO FEEL GOOD

You can lift your spirits in many ways in order to feel good about yourself. Whether you're feeling bad about your weight, your physical appearance, your level of education, your personal image or anything else, you don't have to allow these external things to dictate the way you feel about yourself.

Feelings can be changed by just shifting your perspective as well as your focus. So let's look at some ways you could use right now to do this.

Look for the beauty that's within you

We often look at other people's beauty in admiration - whether it's their physical or inner beauty or their personality. And that's okay. But we all have an inner beauty that's unique to each of us.

And with the same admiration you have for other people's beauty, you need to look at your own beauty. In so doing, you'll begin to feel good about yourself instead of feeling down because the other person has something you wish you possessed.

Help someone

You energy level soars to a higher level when you help other people. The interesting thing about helping others is that you help yourself in return. The rewards are immediate as well as long-lasting. The seeds of your generosity grows forward way into your future and matures into abundant fruit in your life.

Do something creative

What's your talent? What do you enjoy doing? Do something creative - paint a new art piece, write a new song, create a story. Think of something that you can do well and then do it. Don't stop until you've completed it. You'll feel good about your accomplishment and about yourself. Who knows what other creative ideas might emerge in the process.

Express Gratitude

What could you be thankful for right now? You may not be at your ideal weight yet. You may not have the physical appearance you would have preferred to have or you may not have the education you wished you had right now. But you can still express gratitude for what you do have, which may be a whole lot more than what many others don't have.

Can't think of anything? How about being thankful that you're able to read this chapter for starters so you can begin to implement these strategies right away.

And by the way, there are many people who are unable to read or don't have access to the internet or who cannot see to read even if they did have internet access. Think about that for a second and be thankful for what you do have right now.

Exercise and eat well

When you workout you'll find yourself more energized throughout the day and the chemicals being released into your body will automatically begin to help you feel good about yourself.

Eat a well-balanced diet with lots of fruits and vegetables - live foods - that will feed your cells. This not only helps you feel good physically but it will help you feel good emotionally as well.

One thought leads to another and builds on the initial thought. So what else can you do to lift your spirit so you could feel good about yourself?

Changing your life may seem like an overwhelming frustrating process. But it doesn't have to be if you're given simple doable step-by-step strategies that will get you from where you are to where you want to be and experience a transformed life.

CHAPTER 56

CREATE YOUR PERCEPTION WITH PERSONAL BRANDING

Many people say "perception is reality". Wouldn't it be great if you could control and determine how people defined you? Well you can with what has now been coined as personal branding.

Personal branding is self-positioning yourself to become an expert at whatever subject matter you choose. Whether it be technology, relationships, gourmet cooking, or motivational speaking, everything you do must reflect back to that subject in some way, shape, or form.

If you are curious on how to begin crafting your own personal brand here are some self-reflective ways to begin creating one.

Take time to figure out your passion

Write down what you are passionate about and everything you do that promotes this passion. For example, if you are passionate about cooking, you may want to write down how many times you cook meals, how advanced your skills are, if you have created any recipes, if you aspire to be a personal or gourmet chef, etc. All of these speak to why you could begin to be an expert in the field of cooking.

Pinpoint your personality

Figure out what or how you want others to perceive you personality-wise. Are you funny or goofy? Do you like to have deep, intellectual conversations? Do you find joy in giving back to others?

Begin doing things to reflect whatever personality trait you want to focus on and pretty soon people will look to you for a joke, an philosophical thought, or a place to volunteer locally.

But a word to the wise, in order to maintain this personal branding you must actually be interested in whatever personality trait you are trying to convey or people will start to label you as a phony, and you never want that to happen.

Use social media to share your brand with others

Now that we live in the social media and networking age, it is much easier than ever to let others know when and how you're working on your personal brand. If you love cooking, begin hosting dinner parties or offering catering services, start a blog and take pictures of the meals you make and share them on your favorite social networking site.

There are countless different social networking mediums out there, so be careful that the ones you choose to share your brand on are used by the people you want to know you. Some of the most popular ones are Facebook, MySpace, Twitter, and LinkedIn.

Be consistent

If you do not remember anything, please remember this last tip for developing your personal brand-- be consistent. A brand must always send a clear and concise message.

If you fail to keep your personal brand consistent and begin sending send out different messages that have nothing to do with your brand then no one will be able to follow you and confusion will more than likely ensue.

The most important way to keep your brand consistent is by choosing a name you want to be known by and sticking to it. If you are a chef known for your charming ways then your domain name (www.thecharmingchef.com) should be the same as your Facebook name (The Charming Chef), which should also be the same as your twitter name (@TheCharmingChef).

Remember consistency is key

If you want to expand beyond social media to promote your personal brand you may want to consider some of these different methods that are not often talked about but can be just as effective when trying to convey a personal brand:

- Public speaking

- Wardrobe

- Video

- Resume

- Interior Design

- Automobile etc.

CHAPTER 57

TIPS TO HELP YOU GET MOTIVATED

All of us have some form of motivation and it is different for each of us. There are simple things that could motivate us like, buying a really nice pair of shoes, shopping, or simply having some free time. No matter what it is that motivates us, there are certain things that keep us in this motivated state.

Despite your many efforts to succeed in life there are those times that our motivation seems to fall off a cliff. These situations are quite normal and luckily there are easy ways on how to get around them

1) Imagination

If you can think it, it can be done. It's been said that whether you think you can or cannot you are right.

Imagination is our limitless resource of information. It is what drives people to come up of new things to make life better. It is also the starting point for motivation. Imagining how things will begin, the series of coordinated events, and the desired outcomes will most likely fuel anyone's intentions.

On the other hand, there is one twist to this though. We should avoid thinking negative thoughts or contradictory imaginations that may result negatively. Pessimistic imagination can only do so much as bring doubt. It cannot do us any good and would not motivate us at all.

On the other hand, a healthy dose of realizing consequences can be helpful. Just don't bring it to the point that would compromise our entire motivational plot. Think positive and imagine greater thing that will fire up our mood and motivate ourselves.

2) Making Motivation a Habit

Until the very last ounce of life that we breathe, there is hope of achieving great things. Although we may have reached some of our goals, that does not mean that our life is already complete and we do not have any need for motivation.

Let us keep in mind that without motivation, we wouldn't get anywhere. Make motivation an everyday habit. Imagine, reimagine, and live our thoughts. Put this in a constant loop each day and we will find it easy to achieve a better life, reach new heights, and become a far better individual.

3) Start Your Day being Positive

Have you ever woken up in the wrong side of the bed? Most of us have at one time or another and it lasted throughout the day.

If negativity could last from the moment we wake up till we lay to rest at night, so can being positive. Kick start our day with a nice warm smile and a positive attitude. The right mind-set at the right time can be a game changer.

4) Imagine Our Accomplishments

Probably the best way to get ourselves motivated with work is to think about that sweet moment when we've finished each task assigned to us. It's a very delightful feeling when we have accomplished everything and all the burden and stress on our mind just disappears into thin air.

Thinking of that feeling of finishing our tasks will surely enlighten our mood. No matter how boring or tough the task may be, knowing that there's some enlightenment waiting for us at the finish line makes us feel energized, determined, and motivated.

5) Staying Motivated At Work

It's been said that more work gets done on the day before we are due to go on annual leave than any other day, why not make all days as productive and feel great as a result?

There are days that work at the office can be such a drag that by the moment you go out the office door we feel like we've already spent every ounce of our energy.

This normally happens to anyone especially when there are a lot of deadlines to beat, our boss breathing down our neck, and a ton of paperwork. Anyway, we should not be discouraged with these things.

This is quite normal so let's not worry. Work is basically work, so this normally happens almost every day. However, the difference comes on how we look at things. If we look at it closer, those employees at the bottom of the pecking order normally see work as just work.

On the other hand, the CEO's and other higher-ups are somewhat visionaries that see a different side of things which make them the leaders of a company. Earn the way up the food chain by motivating ourselves to do better at work.

6) Get That "Stuck" Feeling

Have you ever imagined yourself glued to your chair? Try this one out and imagine yourself being held down, your back glued to your chair, your feet nailed to the floor, and your only option to escape is to finish your tasks and finish them well. It's a little too much for some but there are just some people who need a little extra motivation than others.

7) Let's Scare Ourselves A Bit

Yes, you read it right. Scaring our self a bit need not be looking at out of this world zombie apocalypse type of scare but rather more realistic approaches like monetary concerns. Imagine our self in a tight situation where bills pile up and our pay isn't due within the next fortnight. A little scare can be a good source of motivation.

Thinking of the consequences can push people beyond their limits. We could harness this feeling even if there's no real monetary concern of any sort. It's like creating a hypothetical problem that can scare us to work better in the real world. It's purely psychological but the results are quite real and their good too.

8) Take Care of Ourselves and keep an eye on Our Health.

Some of the time it's easy to neglect ourselves and the simple things that can motivate us. Personal grooming and health can easily be overlooked which is always a big no. Before we do anything else, we need to be sure to put our personal welfare on top of the list.

It's not being greedy or anything but rather giving ourselves assurance that if anything goes wrong, we can move on any time. Buy ourselves a new suit, a nice looking tie, and a pair of good looking shoes or trainers. Investing in our self never hurts and it retains motivation.

Workouts, and a healthy diet, to keep our bodies physically fit. The very first thing that we should not overlook is our body. One good confidence booster is by having good health. Nothing beats a nice looking healthy body that we and others seeing you would like. Getting in shape would definitely give us a head start.

9) Find out What Easily Bothers Us

There are certain things that bother us most of the time. These are those little things that make us experience that unbearable itch that really annoys us. Find out what it is and take time to realize the situation and come up with a plan to keep it from coming back.

10) Rid Yourself of Negativity

The most dangerous thing that we could ever come up with would be negativity. It's too damaging, stressful, and a complete waste of time. On the other hand, it's a lot easier to get think negatively than positive. Being disappointed in something can stir up a lot of negative thoughts and doubts.

We should never be negative because it will only steer us away from our goals. Other than that, negative thinking can drain the life out of us and that's not just our mental health at risk but our physical health as well.

11) Motivation

One aspect of the formula to success is motivation. The force that propels us to do what's necessary is our undying motivation. Finding that drive to earn success is relatively important as the act of doing. Once we declare it in our minds then we could do it in the real world.

Motivation is a key to success but it is not alone. Motivation in its own self is useless without other correlating factors that make up the whole picture. However, having the inspiration to do things is already much of an achievement but it still is not complete.

12) Commitment and Determination

Pursuing a goal is not all about motivation. Although motivation plays a huge part in the pursuit of a goal but it alone cannot act on itself. It must be met with equal amounts of determination and commitment.

To get hold of that success that we seek, we must commit ourselves to reaching those goals, being determined along the way, and having the motivation to drive ourselves from start to finish. Whether it's success in work, business, or in school, a combination of these three elements is always necessary.

13) Finally Be Happy With What We Do

Excellence can be achieved if we find the joy to work. The best way of doing something is by enjoying it. While reaching our goals, enjoy and take pleasure with whatever it is that we are doing. It is then and only then can we can reach excellence and find joy in our work.

The best people in history were never forced to do something that they did not want. They did it for the love of what they do. They had passion, motivation, sheer determination, and commitment. We could also apply this to ourselves.

Everything starts with us and we start with the motivation to reach our goals. We then reach our goal with the burning passion, determination to move and the commitment to succeed in life. The most important thing of all is not the money or our career but rather the happiness that we felt from start to finish. Enjoy ourselves.

That's a mandatory approach that we should not overlook. Although pressure and stress may always accompany us, don't let them hinder our happiness. It's the ultimate incentive that we can get in this life. Motivate our self through happiness.

However we may define it, being happy is one of the most powerful motivational techniques since the existence of man. After all, if we are living our lives without happiness, we are not living life at all. Let's be happy, feel motivated, and enjoy the beauty of what life has to offer.

CHAPTER 58

KEY PRINCIPLES TO JUMP-START YOUR LIFE AGAIN

These 20 simple, but key principles will jump-start your life again; give you new energy, excitement, passion and leap you forward from where you are now to where it is that you want to go, faster than you ever dared to dream.

1 - Burning Desire

"Success is focusing the full power of all you are on what you have a burning desire to achieve." - Wilfred Peterson

The first principle of goal setting is to have a burning desire. This is not something that you can train yourself to have, you either have it or you don't. You may be able to stay focused on your task or goal for a short time, but without a burning desire you will inevitably lose steam.

2 - Have One Major Goal

(In each area of your life - spiritual, financial, health, etc.)

"There is one quality which one must possess to win, and that is definiteness of purpose, the knowledge of what one wants, and a burning desire to possess it." - Napoleon Hill

About 95% of all Americans do not have goals. Out of the remaining 5% of Americans that do have goals, most set too many goals. Why is this a problem?

Because without one major definite purpose or goal you have no clarity; you are no closer to accomplishing any of your goals than the 95% of Americans that don't set goals at all. Your goals must be clear and specific.

3 - Set Goals that are Achievable Yet Stretch You

"You have to set goals that are almost out of reach. If you set a goal that is attainable without much work or thought, you are stuck with something below your true talent and potential." - Steve Garvey

So many times we do one of two things while setting goals: we either set our goals too high or too low; rarely do we set them just right. This element of goal setting can be extremely difficult, especially without much experience using this process.

By setting our goals too low we never reach our full potential to what we can accomplish and never live a self-fulfilling life. By setting our goals too high we risk becoming discouraged because the goal is so far out of reach.

4 - Set Goals that are Measurable

"Determine a single measure that you can use to grade your progress and success in each area of your life. Refer to it daily." - Brian Tracy

Goals are to be measurable solely for the benefit of being able to track your progress. It is no different than tracking your progress while driving your car to work. When you drive your car to work you know how far you've gone and how far you need to go.

It is simply not enough to say, "I want to be physically fit." How will you know if you are physically fit? Try instead being more specific, an example of this might be, "I run a 7 minute mile". It's clear, precise, and measurable.

5 - Write Down Your Goals

"Write it down. Written goals have a way of transforming wishes into wants, cant's into cans, dreams into plans, and plans into reality. Don't just think it - ink it." -

Be sure that when you write down your goal it is clear, positive, and in present tense. An example of this is, "I earn $100,000 per year". By simply writing down your goal you are making it become alive; you are making your goal a reality.

6 - Set an Achievement Date

"Goals are dreams with deadlines" - Diana Scharf Hunt

Parkinson's Law says, "Work expands so as to fill the time available for its completion." The more time we give ourselves to accomplish a task or goal, the more time it takes us to accomplish it. Therefore, we must learn to use Parkinson's Law to our advantage by setting shorter time frames in which to complete the goal or task.

7 - Identify All Possible Roadblocks and Setbacks

"When you confront a problem you begin to solve it." - Rudy Giuliani

Identifying roadblocks should not discourage you but help you avoid any unexpected setbacks that may occur; enabling you to create the most effective plans possible. By recognizing obstacles your mind should then begin to think of solutions to solve these possible situations.

8 - Create Your Key Indicators

"First you write down your goal; your second job is to break down your goal into a series of steps, beginning with steps which are absurdly easy." - Fitzhugh Dodson

An example of a key indicator is the number of cold calls that you will make. After deciding the key indicator you set a goal for that specific key indicator.

This step is to help you identify the most important tasks that need to be done on a daily basis that bring you closer to accomplishing your goal. By doing what needs to be done first and seeing that task to the end, you will actually spend 80% less time on that task than if you tried doing the same task in smaller increments.

9 - Make Plans

"Planning is bringing the future into the present so that you can do something about it now." - Alan Lakein

Trying to accomplish a goal with no plan is like trying to build a skyscraper without first taking the time to map out the blueprints. Without blueprints the construction process will be slow, frustrating, and extremely expensive.

The same also applies to your goal; if you don't take the time to make plans, then accomplishing your goal will be slow, frustrating, and expensive. The cost may not always be in monetary value, but in time wasted, broken relationships, etc. Make plans so that you can begin to create the future you want now.

10 - Be organized

"In this world no one rules by love; if you are but amiable, you are no hero; to be powerful, you must be strong, and to have dominion you must have a genius for organizing." - John Henry Newman

If you are to have dominion over your own life you must be organized; and to truly be organized you must be organized in each and every single way of your life. If your physical surroundings are cluttered then so will be your mind.

So be sure when you sit down to do planning or accomplish a task that your workspace is spotless. If there's papers that you can't do anything about then put them on the floor temporarily and get to work.

11 - Use Leverage

"Give me a lever long enough and a fulcrum on which to place it, and I shall move the world." - Archimedes

Leverage is the ability to exert minimal effort for maximal achievement. An example of this is "OPK" or in other words, other people's knowledge. One of the greatest ways to use leverage is to seek a mentor. By doing this you save yourself time and money by eliminating the trial and error stage and instead begin seeing results.

By creating a mastermind group you leverage several other's knowledge along with their resources and networks helping you reach even more people that could potentially help you reach your goal.

12 - Motivate Yourself to be Disciplined

"Desire is the key to motivation, but it's determination and commitment to an unrelenting pursuit of your goal - a commitment to excellence - that will enable you to attain the success you seek." - Mario Andretti

Think of reasons to accomplish your goal rather than excuses not to do them. As you do the tasks that you hate but bring you closer to your goal you will feel more satisfaction, accomplishment, and peace in your life.

It will be difficult at times to keep pushing forward, especially if you do not see results immediately; keep going anyway. A great way to do this is to remind yourself of why you want to accomplish your goal and to always keep the end in mind.

13 - Accountability

"When performance is measured, performance improves. When performance is measured and reported, the rate of improvement accelerates." - Thomas S. Monson

This is why participating in a mastermind group can be so beneficial; it gives us someone to report to who will not only encourage our progress, but hold us accountable for what remains to be done on achieving our goals and related indicators. Remember, the more accountability, the greater the results.

14 - Autosuggestion

"Your ability to use the principle of autosuggestion will depend, very largely, upon your capacity to concentrate upon a given desire until that desire becomes a burning obsession." - Napoleon Hill

Autosuggestion is a process by which an individual trains the subconscious mind to believe something, or systematically schematizes the person's own mental associations, usually for a given purpose.

One way of utilizing autosuggestion is by simply writing down a few statements such as, "I earn $100,000 per year" on an index card, and carry that card at all times.

Whenever the moment arises, first thing in the morning, before retiring to bed, on break at work, etc-- begin reciting what you have written on the card with conviction and an inner belief that what you are saying (have written on the card) about yourself is true.

Keep the statements positive and in the present tense because the subconscious mind sees in pictures. For instance, if you were to say, "I am debt free," the subconscious would only see "debt" and therefore would focus on obtaining more "debt."

A positive, present tense autosuggestion for this idea could be, "I am financially independent" or "Money flows to me easily."

15 - Take Action

Do not wait; the time will never be "just right." Start where you stand, and work with whatever tools you may have at your command, and better tools will be found as you go along. - Napoleon Hill

Often times we say that we will accomplish our lifetime goals after we accomplish some other less important goals. Remember, there is never a better time than right now to do something, no matter what it is.

America did not gain its freedom by waiting for the "right time", and neither will you. Why not begin today on making a better life for yourself and loved ones?

16 - Failure is Not an Option

"In achieving your goals, you may run into roadblocks. Don't let that stop you, go around, over, or under. If you are committed to your goal you will find a way." - Catherine Pulsifier

By deciding from the very beginning that failure is not an option you set yourself up for success. Use your desire and drive to accomplish your goal; imagine how wonderful your life will be with the completion of your goal.

Or perhaps contemplate the opposite: how unfulfilled and stressful your life is without it. Regardless of the method of motivation, you must never quit trying to reach your goal.

17 - Stay Positive

"Life's ups and downs provide windows of opportunity to determine your values and goals. Think of using all obstacles as stepping stones to build the life you want." - Martha Sinetar

Despite all the previous steps that you've followed to prevent any roadblocks from showing up on your path to success you will still inevitably run into them. But I have one piece of advice for you: don't get discouraged.

Recognize that every set back and obstacle is an opportunity for improvement and learning. Recognize the benefits of being where you are right now: whether it's learning how to budget or live a healthy lifestyle; there is a positive to every situation.

18 - Reward Yourself

"Reward yourself. Not just the end goal do we celebrate. But each and every little milestone you complete along the way are successes within themselves." - Author Unknown

It is important to reward yourself a minimum of once a week for a job well done. Not only do you get to see the fruits of your labor by doing this, but by taking the time to relax you become more effective and excited about life.

Your rewards do not have to be anything tangible; it can be taking time off work, taking a walk around the park, or enjoying a luxurious bubble bath. The possibilities are endless and deciding on how to reward yourself is half the fun.

19 - Evaluate

"Even if we fail, we can evaluate what we have tried, see what we have done wrong, modify our method of attack - and try again." - John Cusworth

Whether you achieved your goal or not is unimportant, but what is important is to take time to reflect back on all the things that you did to get as far as you did. Ask yourself, "What did I do right?" and "What could I have done better?"

By honestly answering these questions you will already be much further ahead on your next major goal than you were on your previous one, and you will begin to find that each major goal you set will become easier and easier to obtain until it becomes almost effortless.

20 - Make Changes

"The definition of insanity is doing the same thing over and over again and expecting different results." - Albert Einstein

After you've honestly evaluated yourself it's time to make changes. Sometimes they're small and easy adjustments, other times it can be painfully difficult. But if you desire to keep progressing and live a more fulfilling life, then changes must be made constantly.

CHAPTER 59

GET MOTIVATED BY MOTIVATING OTHERS

Motivation is a driving force that directs you to behave or act in a specific manner. It may mean the difference between failure and success or even a good day and a bad day at the office. Did you wake up with that dreaded feeling of being on a slump?

Don't worry, even the most motivated person you know, will go down that road once or twice in his or her lifetime. The important thing is to find that driving force so you can get up and continue reaching for your goals. Good thing motivation isn't really hard to find these days or is it?

Goal-Based Social Networks

Social networks have changed the way people communicate. It has also become a venue for motivating others. How many times have you logged in on Facebook or Twitter and found someone motivating another? How many times have you seen inspirational posts or a well-meaning "you can do it!" comment on an otherwise depressing status update?

Sure, you might say it takes more than a simple tweet or status update to get a person motivated. However, if you are on a slump, a boost to your morale could create a big difference. This is especially true if the boosts come from people you care about or experts who understand your situation and are willing to help you get back on track.

Motivating others through social networks have become really common that you'll now find goal-based social networks, whose main aims are to help you set smart goals and promote effective goal management.

With experts coming to your aid and trying to make things easier for you to reach your goal, it won't be difficult to find the motivation you need to carry on. If others care enough about your goals, wouldn't you be pushed to keep on going?

What Comes Around Goes Around

Goal-based social networks promote a nurturing environment. As others help you get motivated, you'll want to motivate others too. It's a cycle - and a positive one that is. The more you get involved in the network, the more you'll find reasons to achieve your goals and share your new found drive with others.

A goal-based social network is not just another networking site. You won't just see your network expand. You will be able to create meaningful relationships with others. Through these relationships, you will have the chance to inspire and be inspired by connections.

For motivation, why not share your goals and speak with mentors so you may learn better ways to achieve your goals. To motivate others, don't forget to share your success and inspire people to do the same.

If you're on a slump, you don't have to go too far to look for motivation. Visit a goal-based social network and join the bandwagon of individuals who would like to create positive changes in other people's lives.

It won't be long before you find yourself waking up with zest and ticking off one goal after another. Soon, you'll be motivating others as they start seeing how you are able to reach your goals and by letting them know that if you can do it, they can too.

CHAPTER 60

MOTIVATION THROUGH SELF AFFIRMATIONS

Motivation through self affirmation is the concept in which someone re-affirms a desired change their thoughts or a personal attribute. A self affirmation is a tool used to change, inspire, and motivate ones thoughts and view of one's self. A self affirmation is a word or phrase encouraging you to focus on what you want or how you would like to change.

An easy self affirmation is not focusing on our current situation in order to elicit change. An example of this would be, "I don't want to be stressed." By saying what you do not want will actually affirm your negative thoughts and you will possibly attracts more stress.

Here are some examples of other phrases you do not want consider: 1. I don't want to be overweight. 2. I don't want to be negative. 3. I don't want to be a bad boss.

An easy affirmation is a reinforcement of what change you want to elicit. A good example would be, "I am in control of my life." When determining your change see yourself as already being changed by using an easy self help motivator such as," I am."

Here are some examples of easy self affirmations: 1. I am thin. 2. I am a positive person. 3. I am a great boss.

Though you may not be thin, positive or a great boss currently but continued reinforcement will help direct you to your desired attribute. Positive thoughts will attract positive results in the same way negative thoughts attract more negativity.

You might have heard the phrase, "opposites attract." While this is true regarding laws of electro magnetism it is not true with our relationships. Think about a day when you were feeling very positive. Were you attracted to someone who was being negative?

Chances are you were not because any attraction towards the negative person may have changed your whole attitude towards the negative. Now if you were in the presence of a positive person you would likely be drawn towards this person as you were inspired by the same positive energy.

Use these easy self help motivational affirmations on a daily basis. Display your affirmations where you will see them throughout your day. Ensure you see the affirmations when you first wake-up and before you go to sleep. This will start and end your day with positive reinforcement of the affirmations and you will elicit change.

Start changing your life by taking one small step towards motivation goals through easy self affirmations.

CONCLUSION

We have gone through the motivating process of envisioning our future and setting goals to get us there. But all of this energy and effort is usually wasted in the end. The Achilles heal of the goal setting process is that we fail to stay focused.

Climbing a mountain is much like goal setting. You pick your mountain, and then plan out a detailed route to the top. But after that, making progress comes down to a very simple principle. You have to place one foot after another, stay on course and you will reach the top.

Our challenge is not picking the mountain, or planning the route, our challenges are staying motivated and on track long enough to get to the top. There are two issues here, the first is all about prioritizing, and the second is about motivation.

The secret of a successful life is the ability to identify your most important tasks, and then stick to them. Often are most important tasks are actually dull and mundane.

Most mountains are reached by taking thousands of mundane steps, and the same is true with our goals. Whenever you set a goal you have to break it down into smaller steps, but remember not all steps are equal.

The ability to distinguish between better and best is one of the most underrated talents in the world. They say 'good' is the enemy of 'great.' This is true when it comes to your priorities as well. You have to identify what is most important and then you have to make sure that those items always take precedence.

One of the best things you can do for yourself on your journey of self discovery is to work out what drives you. The first step is to identify your values as they provide the fuel for your motivation and the drive behind everything you do in life.

If you set goals that are aligned with your values, you will have the motivation to help you achieve them. If you set goals that are not in line with your values, it will be an uphill struggle to achieve them.

When you understand your values and their impact on how you are currently motivating yourself you will have a wonderful insight into why you achieve the results that you do in life. You will also know how to motivate yourself more effectively in the future.

Best wishes!

Made in the USA
Middletown, DE
14 November 2018